THE GREAT MYSTERIES OF ARCHAEOLOGY

A DAVID & CHARLES BOOK

David & Charles is an F+W
Publications Inc. company
4700 East Galbraith Road
Cincinnati, OH 45236

First published in the UK
in 2007

© 2007 E-ducation.it, Firenze
A SCALA Group company
www.e-ducation.it
info@e-ducation.it

This 2007 edition published
by David and Charles
by arrangement with
E-ducation.it.

A catalogue record for this
book is available from the
British Library.

ISBN-13: 978-0-7153-2761-6
paperback
ISBN-10: 0-7153-2761-5
paperback

Printed in China
for David & Charles
Brunel House   Newton
Abbot   Devon

Visit our website at
www.davidandcharles.co.uk

David & Charles books
are available from all good
bookshops; alternatively you
can contact our Orderline on
0870 9908222 or write to
us at FREEPOST EX2 110,
D&C Direct, Newton Abbot,
TQ12 4ZZ (no stamp required
UK only); US customers call
800-289-0963 and Canadian
customers call 800-840-5220.

Project Director: Cinzia Caiazzo
Editor-in-chief: Filippo Melli
Texts: Maria Rosaria Luberto
Editorial Staff: Giulia
Marrucchi, Sibilla Pierallini
Captions: Francesca Taddei
Graphics: Maria Serena Di
Battista
Translation: Johanna Kreiner

Photographs:
© 2007 Archivio Fotografico
SCALA GROUP
© Foto Scala Firenze/HIP
© SCALAGROUP and COREL
All rights reserved.
© Foto Werner Forman
Archive/Scala, Firenze

© Bridgeman Art Library/Alinari
© Corbis: © José Fuste Raga/
Corbis; © Kazuyoshi Nomachi/
Corbis; © Gian Berto Vanni/
Corbis; © Wolfgang Kaehler/
Corbis; © Charles & Josette
Lenars/Corbis; © Tibor Bognár/
Corbis; © Thomas Hartwell/
Corbis
© DeAgostini: © C. Sappa/
DeAgostini; © S. Vannini/
DeAgostini
© Photoservice Electa/Jemolo
© Jürgen Liepe -
Ägyptisches Museum und
Papyrussammlung/BPK
© Gloria Rosati

Illustrations, selected from
the Scala Archives, of property
belonging to the Italian Republic
are published by concession
of the competent authority
(Ministero per i Beni e le Attività
Culturali).

THE GREAT MYSTERIES OF ARCHAEOLOGY

THE PYRAMIDS

David and Charles

TABLE OF CONTENTS

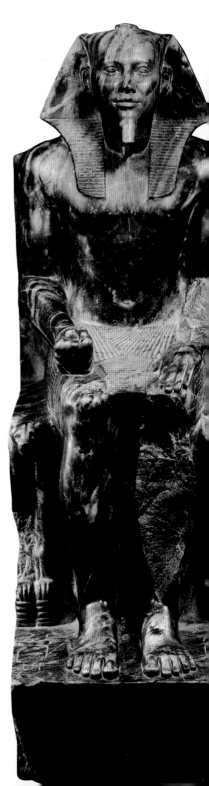

Louis Haghe, *View of the Pyramids of Giza from the Nile*, c. 1845, British Library, London.

THE DISCOVERY

Symbols of ancient Egypt and icons of eternity, the pyramids trace their impressive silhouette against the flat background of the desert. Their apparently perfect geometry is somehow reassuring, but the outward simplicity of these stone giants is only the shell of a reality that has remained unfathomable. These enormous angular structures have fascinated scholars and enthusiasts of all epochs, as the numerous accounts by ancient Greek and Roman writers, as well as the records of medieval caliphs (Islamic rulers) and the Napoleonic projects all reveal. The explorations and discoveries of more recent times have certainly deepened our knowledge about them, though they have not yet resolved even one of the many enigmas of these monuments.

The Giza Pyramids through History

Pyramids of Giza, c. 2570-2520 BC. Their enigmatic character fascinated the ancient Greeks and Romans.

In ancient times the Greeks and Romans were profoundly fascinated by the sealed and inaccessible pyramids. Even then there were no Egyptians who could explain the meaning and the function of these amazing structures. The first writings to reveal a serious interest in these monuments come from the Greek historian Herodotus, who saw the Khufu Pyramid (often known as the Cheops Pyramid or

Great Pyramid) in the 5th century BC, from Diodorus Siculus (1st century BC), and from the geographer Strabo who visited Egypt in the year 30 BC with the expedition of the Roman consul Gaius Aelius Gallus. They all believed that the pyramids were royal tombs, although none of them could claim to know the names of their occupants with any certainty.

The first real exploration of a pyramid, that of Khufu, took place in the year 820 AD, according to the account that the Arab historian Al-Ma'sūdī narrated in his *Universal History*, a twenty-volume work of which only one survives (in the Library of Vienna). In that year, Caliph Al-Ma'mūn visited the pyramids, became convinced that they must have contained immense treasures, and decided to seize them at all costs.

In the adventure-packed story, Al-Ma'sūdī told how the

Colossal head, probably representing Khufu, 3rd millennium BC, Brooklyn Museum of Art, New York.

12 THE PYRAMIDS

caliph's workmen opened a passageway by using vinegar, fire and levers, and that they found their way into a pit that contained a pot of gold, the value of which was exactly equal to the expenses of the caliph to finance the operation.

The shrewd author praised the genius of the ancients who had been so clairvoyant as to foresee exactly how much the caliph would have spent to reach that point and had left the treasure for him!

According to other authors, it was not Al-Ma'mūn who first opened the pyramids but his father, Caliph Harūn-el-Rashīd, the protagonist of the *Thousand and One Nights*. They say that it was only after unbelievable labours that he was finally able to enter the structure, which was full of pits and tunnels, and that he reached a chamber 'in the shape of a cube' with a marble sarcophagus at the

View of the tombs of the caliphs, the first to penetrate inside the pyramids. Cairo.

centre, which he ordered to be removed. Inside he found a decomposed body. The expenses for this expedition were so high that Caliph Harūn-el-Rashīd decreed that no other pyramids would be opened, and in fact none were.

During the 12th century another Arab writer recorded: 'They say that in Al-Ma'mūn's time a man had entered (the Khufu Pyramid) and reached a small chamber where there was a statue of a man in green stone like malachite.

The statue was carried away by Al-Ma'mūn; it had a lid and when it was raised they found the body of a man inside wearing a golden cuirass encrusted with gems of all kinds.'

According to the same source, the caliph had dug a corridor, which led to a room where two galleries came together. At the centre a pit led to other subterranean chambers full of skeletons and bats, while another gallery went upwards.

The story of the opening of the pyramids by Al-Ma'mūn is referred in works by

Joseph's Granaries

During the 14th century a legend evolved that the pyramids had originally been used as immense granaries at the time of the great famine, as narrated in the Bible (Genesis, 39-50), which only Egypt had survived without suffering thanks to its viceroy, Joseph the Jew.

The success of this interpretation is documented by the fact that the pyramids are depicted with this function in the decorations of one of the domes of the St Mark's Basilica in Venice. During the 9th century, however, the Patriarch of Antioch, Denys de Tell-Mahré, had already expressed a different opinion and affirmed that the pyramids were 'extraordinary mausoleums erected over [...] hidden, solid tombs, not hollow and empty'.

The most sophisticated and learned of the medieval pilgrims also realized that they must have been monuments to someone or something rather than granaries. In fact a Florentine traveller of the 14th century, Giorgio di Messer Guccio Gucci wrote: 'We went to see the granaries of the Pharaoh [...] lined up three by three. These granaries [...] they say the Pharaoh made them [...] at the time of Joseph; but looking at them they seem more likely to have been made for perpetual memory than granaries'. It is surprising that Gucci's travelling companion, Lionardo di Niccolò Frescobaldi, remained faithful to the traditional interpretation in his own writings, even though he had read and taken many hints from his colleague's account: 'In the region of Cairo [...] there are 13 granaries that Joseph had built at the time of the king Pharaoh king of Egypt in the days of the great famine, these are still standing [...] and are still under a lot of earth'.

several Arab authors, mostly contemporary to authors cited here. All of them, despite the colourful details added to the individual versions, mention the excavation of a tunnel at the caliph's orders and the finding of a body, whether mummified and wearing royal garments according to some, or naked and decomposed according to others.

Later, archaeologists actually found traces of these incursions that continued through the centuries. The repeated thefts involved both the contents inside the pyramids, and the stones themselves as construction material for other buildings.

From about 1200 the blocks of the pyramids were in fact used to build the palaces of the caliphs and the walls of the fortress at Cairo. These operations were so popular that eventually a tax was imposed for making use of materials from the pyramids.

VENDEBA EGY...

Joseph orders distribution of grain, mosaic. St Mark's Basilica, Venice.

The pyramids in the background are represented as granaries.

The Seven Wonders of the World

The ancients included the Giza pyramids among the 'Seven Wonders of the World', the seven works of art and architecture of the ancient world that were considered the most outstanding. This unusual list was handed down by Diodorus Siculus (1st century BC), but it seems the list was originally compiled at Alexandria in Egypt between 304 and 292 BC.

The classification included, in the following order:

1. The Lighthouse of Alexandria of the 3rd century BC, built on the island of Pharos, which gave its name to the lighthouse in many languages.

2. The Colossus of Rhodes, a statue about 36 metres high, built by the inhabitants as an offer to their sun god, Helios, for having saved them from a siege.

3. The Mausoleum at Halicarnassus, a funeral temple built by Maussollos (who gave his name to this type of structure) for his remains after death, which took place in 362 BC.

4. The Temple of Artemis at Ephesus, designed by Theodorus of Samos and financed by the legendary Lydian king Croesus during the 6th century BC; destroyed by a fire, it was rebuilt in 333 BC.

5. The lost statue of Zeus at Olympia (5th century BC), a chryselephantine sculpture (gold for the hair, garments and sandals; ivory for the exposed parts of the body) fashioned by Phidias; the statue was some 12 metres high and the floor of the cell where it stood had to be lowered to fit it in.

6. The Hanging Gardens of Babylon, built during the 6th century BC by Nebuchadnezzar for his beloved Semiramis; the exact location has not yet been identified.

7. The Pyramids of Giza.

Before Napoleon

From the end of the 13th century the flow of visitors to the land of the pyramids became relentless. Most of them were traders and government officials who travelled to Egypt for work, but they never failed to go to Giza and leave their impressions, more or less detailed, for our benefit.

In 1512 a group of emissaries from Venice reached Egypt. Zaccaria Pagani was among them: in his travel notes he mentioned that in the pyramid of Khufu he had seen 'an empty, open sarcophagus of porphyry [which authorized the hypothesis that the site] had been the tomb of a king of Egypt'.

No doubt his interpretation was correct, but the fact that he proposed it as a hypothesis suggests that at the time there were many other theories about the matter, despite the discovery of sarcophagi inside the pyramids.

In the *Encyclopédie* by
Diderot and d'Alembert
(1751-76) the pyramids
were described as
monuments conceived
by the Egyptians on which
they would write the great
events of their history.

During the following
centuries many other visitors,
both enthusiasts and travel
writers, went to the sites, but
it was only after 1798 that
the scientific study of these
monuments began.

Pyramids
of Egypt,
an illustration
from
*Cosmografia
Universale*
by Sebastian
Munster,
Basel, 1554;
Bibliothèque
Nationale, Paris.

The Birth of Egyptology

In July 1798, a commission of scholars arrived in Alexandria with the expedition of Napoleon Bonaparte. Their mission was to study the culture and civilization of Egypt carefully, with particular attention to the ancient world. The Commission of Arts and Sciences which included, as the name suggests, all the arts and the scientific disciplines, was guided by Dominique Vivant Denon under the burning rays of the sun, through sand storms and violent incidents, to analyze, measure and record calculations about every sort of monument they found. The scholars also collected archaeological finds and samples of rocks and plants, amidst the general scorn of the escorting soldiers who could not understand risking their lives for such a purpose. The outcome of the expedition was a publication with a rather ringing title, *Description de l'Egypt ou Recueil des observations et des recherches qui ont été faites en Egypte pendant l'expédition de l'armée français* (Description of Egypt: collected observations and research carried out during the French military expedition). Four volumes of text (out of nine) and five volumes of illustrations (out of twelve) were dedicated to archaeology and contained, in addition to the description of the monuments and significant sites, all the calculations, sketches and measurements carried out by the commission. During the expedition, Colonel Coutelle and the architect Le Père were commissioned to systematically explore the most famous of the Egyptian pyramids. Together with 150 Egyptian workers and 100 French soldiers, they proceeded to free the pyramid of Khufu, which had been opened during the Middle Ages, from the sand that surrounded it, and to remove debris from the interior, including the chamber known as the Grand Gallery. An unexpected order to retreat prevented them from finishing

Opposite: Interior of the pyramid of Unas. Walls inscribed with the *Texts of the Pyramids*, c. 2323 BC, Saqqara. The first scientific exploration of Egyptian monuments was carried out by the scholars who accompanied Napoleon's expedition to Egypt.

Rosetta Stone, 196 BC, British Museum, London. The discovery of this stone made it possible to decipher hieroglyphics.

a part of their project: the dismantling of one of the pyramids. Nevertheless, one effect of the mysterious fascination of these buildings was that a section of the Egypt Institute, founded by Napoleon, was dedicated to the study of ancient buildings in the landscape.

This series of important studies stirred up great enthusiasm in Europe, even though the intellectual disciplines, the methods and the instruments for a truly scientific investigation were still not fully developed. For example, in 1818, an abbot whose cousin was the Director of the museums of France, proposed to celebrate Mass on the platform of a pyramid in order to exalt the triumph of the Christian god over the pagan gods! The real turning point, and the birth of Egyptology, in the sense of the critical study and analysis of the monuments and documents of ancient Egypt, happened quite casually. In 1799 a soldier of Napoleon's army discovered the famous Rosetta stone, on which

a decree of Ptolemy V is engraved in three languages: hieroglyphics, Greek and demotic, the common script of ancient Egypt. In 1808 a copy of the inscription was sent to François Champollion, a scholar whose comparative studies enabled him, in 1822, to decipher hieroglyphic script. This important breakthrough made it possible to collect much more information about Egypt and its inhabitants, contained in numerous surviving documents of various types. However there was only one subject about which information was still scarce: the pyramids, naturally. This led to the strangest speculations about the nature and the function of the pyramids, so not even the early explorations served to restore a serious tone to the discussions.

Pyramids of Gizeh.
July 17th 1839.   David Roberts R.A.

Louis Haghe, *The Sphinx and the Pyramids on the Plain of Giza*, c. 1842-1849. British Library, London. This is how the Sphinx appeared when it was surrounded by sand.

Ippolito Rosellini

Born in Pisa in 1800, Ippolito Rosellini had a short but intense and productive life completely dedicated to the study of Egyptian civilization. After taking his degree in theology, he obtained a professorship of ancient Oriental studies and languages at the University of Pisa. His meeting with Champollion was decisive for the development of his career. After overcoming a series of obstacles, the Franco-Tuscan expedition, prepared and guided by the two scientists, set sail for Egypt on 31 July 1828. Over the course of a year the expedition had sailed up the Nile as far as the second cataracts. Along the way they had copied all the hieroglyphic inscriptions they found and, at the same time, divided the finds from the excavations between the Egyptian Museum of Florence and the Louvre in Paris. When they returned home in 1829, Champollion died and Rosellini was forced to review the great quantity of materials they had collected alone. This work resulted in a three-volume report entitled *The Monuments of Egypt and Nubia*, the last volume of which was published posthumously after the premature death of the author in June 1843.

THE BEGINNING OF THE TREASURE HUNT

In Europe, the Napoleonic expedition and the decipherment of hieroglyphic script inspired a great passion for Egyptian culture. European diplomats resident in Egypt began to collect archaeological finds and send them to their own countries, thus creating the bases of the Egyptian museum collections in Turin, Paris, Berlin and London.

The era of the great scientific expeditions was launched, which began to bring the culture of ancient Egypt to light. The British government played an especially important role, through its consuls and their contacts with British businessmen, soldiers and adventurers. The English consuls became an integral part of the history of the Giza plain: first, Henry Salt; followed by Patrick Campbell, Colonel Richard William Howard Vyse, and the engineer John Perring (who worked for Campbell in Egypt from 1836 to 1839).

Italy also participated in the scientific fervour of this period through two controversial figures: the traveller Giovanni Battista Caviglia, and the adventurer Giovanni Battista Belzoni, who worked for Consul Henry Salt.

In the meantime, in 1828, the great Franco-Tuscan expedition departed for Egypt. It was the result of a productive encounter between Champollion, who had gone to Italy to examine the materials in an Egyptian collection, and Ippolito Rosellini, the father of Italian Egyptology.

The expedition was made possible by the joint financing provided by King Charles X of France and the Grand Duke of Tuscany, Leopold II.

Opposite: Giuseppe Angelelli, *The Franco-Tuscan Expedition in Egypt*. Archaeological Museum, Florence. Champollion is seated at the centre, Rosellini is standing next to him.

From Egyptology to Egyptomania

The great curiosity about Egyptian culture and civilization attracted crowds of tourists and scholars, or people pretending to be scholars, to the banks of the Nile in an intense and self-defeating treasure hunt. While Egyptology was developing, Europe was invaded by an overwhelming taste for Egypt that inspired the styles of clothing and hairstyles, porcelain and tableware, architecture and furnishings. In London the Regency style was born, with the settees in the form of crocodiles or sphinxes created by Thomas Hope, while in Paris, the wave of enthusiasm for the discoveries of the Napoleonic expedition took shape in the Empire style. This wave of fashion touched literature as well: Egypt became the most fascinating topic of conversation in the literary salons, and the subject of many novels set in the land of the Pharaohs, from famous authors such as Gustave Flaubert in his *Voyage to Egypt*, and Théophile Gautier who wrote *Romance of a Mummy*.

Caviglia and the Pyramid of Khufu

In 1817 Giovanni Battista Caviglia, a Genoan navigator and dilettante scientist, with a rather brusque and closed character, continued the exploration of the pyramid of Khufu. The French travelling with Napoleon had stopped excavations at a depth of 16 metres, where even breathing was not a simple matter. Caviglia followed a tortuous path that, in part, followed the traces of the tomb raiders and, after passing through a number of corridors, he found the head of a pit which, when freed of debris, once again permitted air to circulate inside the structure. Caviglia was then joined by Consul Salt and Samuel Briggs, the banker and financer of the undertaking. Together they entered a room between two air ducts they had freed from debris and here, to their amazement, they read Greek and Latin inscriptions from Roman and Byzantine eras, undeniable evidence of the numerous incursions the monument had suffered long

before their arrival. Studies of the pyramid of Khufu picked up again in 1836 with renewed impetus from the new English consul in Cairo, Patrick Campbell, with the assistance of Colonel Howard Vyse. The latter had engaged the engineer John Perring, who immediately began to explore the chambers inside the structure with excellent results but by using

Pyramid of Khufu, c. 2570 BC, Giza. Excavations and exploration during the 19th century made it possible to attribute the monument to Pharaoh Khufu (Cheops).

methods that would make any modern scholar tear his hair, Perring opened his way through the debris by way of dynamite blasts, and he forced the gates that protected the burial chamber with the same tactics. Howard Vyse wrote: 'Every time there was an explosion, the workers had to use a rope ladder to come up because the wooden stairs had been destroyed by the stone chips and the effect of the gunpowder. In the four chambers opened with this very unorthodox system, they were finally able to read the name of the king for whom the building had been created: Khufu (Cheops), an attribution that until this discovery had been founded solely on the words of Herodotus, the Greek historian.

Thomas Milton, *View of the Plain of Giza with the Great Pyramid of Khufu*, c. 1801, British Library, London. This is how the pyramid must have appeared before the 19th-century explorations.

The Almost Untouched Pyramid

Although the pyramid of Khufu had clearly been extensively explored already in ancient times, it seemed that the same was not true for the pyramid of Khafre (Chephren).

This became a real obsession for Giovanni Battista Belzoni, an Italian from Padua who was working for Consul Salt, who did not want to participate in the explorations of the pyramid of Khufu. Belzoni focused his efforts on the search for the entrance to the Khafre Pyramid in his mania to make the great discovery that would make him famous forever: to be the first to enter what seemed to be an untouched tomb. In 1818, accompanied by Giovanni d'Athanasi, a Greek in the service of the English government, he began to concentrate his efforts on the north face, near the point where there seemed to be traces of a tunnel bored by thieves.

He was not mistaken: he found the entrance covered by three enormous blocks of granite that also blocked the descending corridor.

It was not possible to use the corridor because it was full of debris, but the young man did not give up: after only three days of feverish work the passageway was finally free.

His perseverance was rewarded, beyond his hopes, on 2 March 1818, when only one obstacle to the coveted objective, the chamber of the sarcophagus, appeared before him and his workers.

The obstacle was a massive gate of granite that was not completely closed. Giovanni d'Athanasi managed to slip underneath, while the stouter Belzoni had to wait until the whole stone was removed, so despite his ambitions, he was not actually the first to enter the burial chamber.

His joy was quickly dampened when he saw an inscription in Arabic on the

walls of the tomb. Belzoni quickly realized that Khafre's pyramid had not been spared the visits of tomb raiders either, even though he had definitively achieved its re-opening. The evidence is there on the wall of the chamber today: written in large letters with lampblack is Belzoni's name and the date of the event.

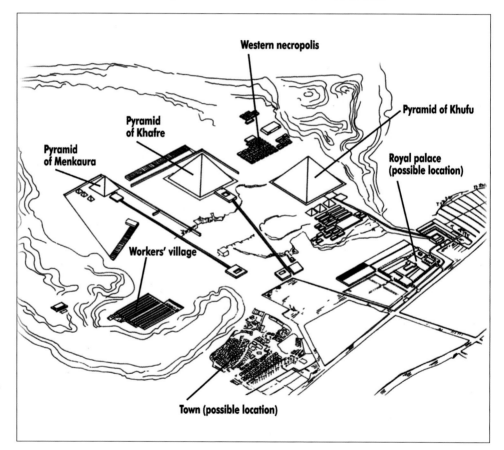

Western necropolis

Pyramid of Khufu

Pyramid of Khafre

Royal palace (possible location)

Pyramid of Menkaura

Workers' village

Town (possible location)

Plan of the pyramid complexes on the plain of Giza (from R. Schulz, M. Seidel, *Egypt*, Cologne 1998, p. 63, fig. 36).

Interior of the
burial chamber
in the pyramid
of Khafre, with
the inscription
of Belzoni's
name and the
date of the re-
opening of the
tomb.

Searching for Menkaura (Mycerinus)

Another of Belzoni's projects, to complete his discoveries, was to enter the third pyramid on the Plain of Giza. He failed, because it was impossible to move the heavy blocks that had originally formed the facing of the pyramid and had been displaced and rolled down during the Middle Ages.

In 1837, however, Howard Vyse, who was directing the exploration of this pyramid on behalf of Consul Campbell, had a brilliant intuition, which reversed the situation.

Assuming that: the burial chamber was not inside the structure but underground, he excavated in the bedrock. Searching below the tunnel opened previously on the north face, after six months of hard work, at about four metres from the base of the pyramid, Vyse found the duct that led to the burial chamber.

Like the other pyramids, it had already been forced open in ancient times. All the passageways into the tomb were completely filled with debris and sand, while the chamber of the sarcophagus was full of stone chips left over from the period when the interiors of the pyramids were used as a quarry for building materials.

It is easy to imagine the disappointment of Vyse and his team when they found the sarcophagus completely empty and moved from its original position, the cover broken and scattered in the

Drawing of the pyramid of Menkaura (from R. Schulz, M. Seidel, *Egypt*, Cologne 1998, p. 68, fig. 45).

Chamber of the sarcophagus

Hall with 26 niches

Storeroom

Upper vestibule

Pyramid of Menkaura, c. 2520 BC, Giza. This pyramid, like those of Khufu and Khafre, was regularly explored during the first half of the 19th century, but had already been raided.

vestibule that led to the tomb. The identification of the tomb was confirmed by the finding of a fragment of a wooden coffin, together with some pieces of wood and bandages, with an inscription of the name Menkaura (Mycerinus), which corresponded to the name handed down by Herodotus.

The coffin was immediately identified as being much more recent than the date of burial of the Pharaoh. Scholars deduced that the priests responsible for the cult of the sovereign, after having restored order following a period of political and social upheaval, had probably provided a new coffin for the mummy, later desecrated again, as the explorers had come to expect.

The colonel collected all the pieces of the coffin together with the remains of vertebrae and ribs, bones of the legs and feet, wrapped in bandages of heavy cloth and saturated with resins, and handed it all to the British Museum.

Together with these finds, another splendid work was supposed to enter the extraordinary collection that already existed in London. It was a very heavy sarcophagus of smooth basalt, without inscriptions but richly decorated.

Perring succeeded in carrying it laboriously out of the pyramid but it was unfortunately lost when the ship carrying it sank.

The Exploration of the Step Pyramid at Saqqara

The ancestor of the pyramids is a structure that unites the characteristics of the ancient royal tombs, the mastaba tombs, with the new architecture of the perfectly geometric pyramids. It is the step pyramid built for the first time at Saqqara by the founder of the Third Dynasty, pharaoh Djoser (Zoser), whose reign closed the Protodynastic period and was followed by the Old Kingdom. It was again an Italian, Girolamo Segato, who began to explore this pyramid in 1820 on behalf of General Heinrich Carl Menu von Minutoli, a Prussian baron who came from a family of Neapolitan origins. After having measured the external dimensions, Segato found a void, a pit, through which it was possible to enter the structure. This opening, later found to be the work of ancient raiders, was a terrible source of frustration and fatigue because the pit continued to fill up with the same sand that the workmen were trying to shovel out. When this work of Tantalus was finally finished, the Italian was able to descend about 15 metres into the pit on a rope, where he found the entrance gallery, again completely obstructed by debris. He worked for three days underground without coming out, under the constant threat of structural collapse, to survey the structure. The results of the underground survey were astounding: a very intricate series of chambers, corridors, ducts, ramps and landings had been excavated in the bedrock at a depth that varied between 2 and 20 metres. They led to the burial chamber, the entrance to which had originally been barred by a slab of granite, as in the Giza pyramids. Like them, it had been smashed to pieces together with the heavy sarcophagus. All around the

Opposite:
Step pyramid
of Djoser,
c. 2650 BC,
Saqqara.
The initial
explorations
were conducted
by the Italian
explorer Segato.

Royal pavilion,
funerary
complex
of Djoser,
c. 2650 BC,
Saqqara. This
extraordinary
complex was
the first in
Egyptian history
to be built
entirely
of stone.

Panel of green
and blue glazed
ceramic, from
the funerary
complex of
Djoser at
Saqqara,
c. 2650 BC.
Egyptian
Museum, Cairo.

burial chamber there was a
series of other cubicles that
Segato was able to crawl
through on hands and knees,
breathing with difficulty, when
finally he reached a room that
was beautifully decorated
with glazed terracotta tiles.
Almost nothing remains of
the marvellous drawings that
Segato made on this occasion,

because they burned during a
fire in his home in Cairo.

Segato and Von Minutoli
interrupted their activities in
1821; ten years later Perring,
the Englishman, after his
successes in the exploration of
the pyramid of Khufu, began to
explore the Saqqara complex.
Continuing the use of rather
unorthodox methods as in

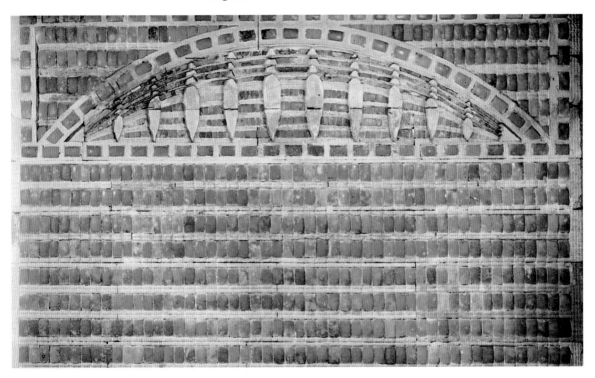

The Prisoners' Heads

Inside the colonnade discovered by Girolamo Segato and reconstructed by Lauer, a sculpture had been found that represented the heads of two prisoners, evidently enemies captured by the Pharaoh. The hair of both subjects is arranged in the same way, with the tresses simply divided into two locks, while the faces are strongly differentiated: the man on the right wears a short goatee beard, while the other has a full beard and moustache which cover his lips, cheeks and chin. This different characterization has led scholars to identify the man on the right as a Libyan and therefore a representative of western peoples, while the man on the left is Asiatic and represents the Orientals.

The representation of defeated enemies under the domination of the pharaoh is a frequent theme in Egyptian art. Even during times of peace this theme was used to represent the order of the universe conserved by the pharaoh of Egypt through his battles and victories over the forces of evil.

Large-scale examples of this type of image were sculpted in the round from blocks that were then used for the sills of doors or windows, pedestals for statues or on the walls of temples and palaces.

In the case of these particular heads, there is no evidence to identify exactly where they were placed, but the fact that the block is split on the left and that the top surface was left unfinished indicates that it was surrounded by other elements, as if in a wall or pedestal.

his previous explorations, he followed an intricate series of passageways and reached, through the pit opened by Segato, a gallery with 22 columns and pilasters with inscriptions. The exceptional find however, was a group of 30 mummies whose presence in that particular location was explained only by later studies.

The structure was actually intended to be a common burial chamber, and had been set up with architectural elements recovered from ruins of other buildings, long after the construction of the pyramid. This interpretation was provided by Jean Philippe Lauer, who also directed the restoration and, to some degree, the reconstruction of the entire complex.

Although these operations were harshly criticized from a scientific point of view, they undoubtedly have contributed to making the monument more comprehensible to the general public.

Opposite: Colonnade, funerary complex of Djoser, c. 2650 BC, Saqqara. The pyramid and the splendid accompanying buildings were created by the famous architect Imhotep, who was later deified.

Sculpture of
two prisoner's
heads, from
the funerary
complex of
Djoser at
Saqqara,
c. 2650 BC,
Egyptian
Museum, Cairo.

An Intricate Puzzle of Riddles

Just about everything has been speculated about the Egyptian pyramids. The difficulty of explaining the structural characteristics, the construction techniques, the symbolic significance of the form, and the lack of information from official Egyptian sources, have since ancient times favoured the proliferation of the most extravagant theories. It has even been suggested that gods came down to earth to reveal secrets to the inhabitants of the Nile valley or that preachers of obscure and esoteric doctrines applied strange theories or magic formulas to these structures.

Greek writers and scholars were the first to wonder about the function of the pyramids, at the time almost completely buried by the desert sands.

In later centuries opinions of all types were expressed until the 15th century, when it was possible to suggest plausible answers to two of the three principle mysteries about them: who had built the pyramids and for what purpose.

It was finally understood that these were monuments erected by the ancient Egyptians to house the pharaohs after death, monuments whose extraordinary characteristics were intended to contribute to the eternal fame of the sovereign. Death, for the Egyptians, was simply

Tombs of the Meroe necropolis in Sudan, 4th century BC–4th century AC. The forms are similar to the pyramids of the Old Kingdom.

considered the beginning of a voyage into the afterlife, and the departure of the pharaoh, who was considered a god on earth, had a special meaning for the entire community.

Considering that the life of his subjects depended on his goodwill, even their afterlives were believed to be intimately related to that of the pharaoh. The pyramids were intended to guarantee that the pharaoh could conduct his voyage with everything he needed and without any danger of desecration. Once these basic concepts were accepted, it was no longer possible to continue talking about granaries, a hypothesis that was quite popular during the 14th century, as mentioned above.

Nonetheless, a series of unsolved mysteries continues to surround these structures,

especially concerning their construction techniques, so that scholars and enthusiasts have and continue to propose a great variety of theories. Limiting the discussion only to the Plain of Giza, where the most studied pyramids stand, the questions that spark the hottest discussions include: when were the pyramids really built? Why did the Egyptians decide not to leave any traces of the construction techniques they used and the methods they used to dress and transport the enormous blocks of stone? How did they acquire all the knowledge required to make the calculations involved in building such monuments? The enigma is even more profound when we consider what is the real significance of the pyramids; what does their form allude to; what are they pointing at?

Book of the Dead, with scenes of the afterlife, Ägyptisches Museum, Berlin. After the 15th century, the pyramids were considered to be the funerary monuments of the pharaohs.

Construction Secrets of the Pyramids: Magic and Science

Model of a procession of porters, Egyptian Museum, Cairo. It is still not clear today how the workers of the period, with so little technology available, were able to construct such colossal buildings as the pyramids.

The workmen carried papers covered with magic script and when a block of stone had been cut and levelled they placed one of these papers on it and struck it once, which was sufficient to move it a distance of 1,000 sahnes (200 arrow shots: 26,000 metres), then they repeated until that stone reached the top of the pyramid: this is how Arab writers of the 14th and 15th centuries explained the mystery of how the pyramids were built! The question of the construction techniques has mystified scholars and enthusiasts since ancient times. Even today, not one of

these colossal blocks of stone is completely understood. One way of fathoming the complexity of what was achieved is by following the steps of work on a typical building site. The first step was to quarry the necessary materials: ordinary quality stone for the internal nucleus, Aswan granite for the more important layers and fine-grained Tura limestone for the external facing. Quarrying

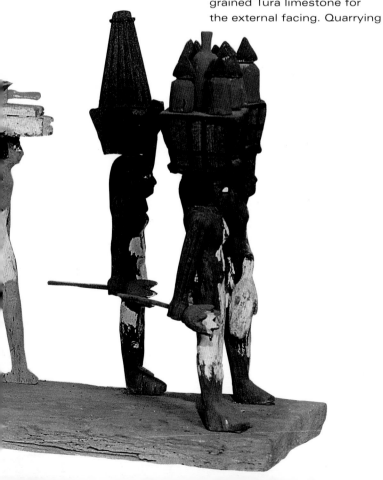

techniques for the first type of stone should not have represented any particular problem for the Egyptians, but how they managed to cut the granite is still not clear today. It is sufficient to recall that today this is done with diamond saw blades (steel with diamond dust), which the Egyptians certainly did not have. Some have hypothesized that they only used blocks that had fallen naturally, but there are signs of wedges on those in the burial chamber of Menkaura, so this explanation seems unlikely.

The only plausible hypothesis would seem to be to beat arrhythmically on the granite with very hard stones to crack it, although such a heavy job would take a considerable time. Some of the materials had to be brought from distances of up to 800 kilometres by sea, on barges or rafts of wood or reeds, or by land on special sleds of wood. But how could the Egyptians transport loads weighing hundreds of tons with such rudimentary means? And how long would it take to transport them such distances? The pyramid of Khufu is composed of 2,300,000 blocks of limestone. Herodotus, the Greek historian affirmed that 100,000 men worked on its construction. Modern archaeologists, who have done some experiments to verify the methods and the time required to complete these titanic undertakings, believe that this number should be reduced to a total of 20,000 men, although they have not succeeded in obtaining definitive results.

Once they reached their destination, these enormous weights had to be raised to great heights: the pyramid of Khufu, for example, is over 147 metres high. There have been countless theories: some suggested that they were moved on rollers made of tree trunks, while others suggested that spiral ramps surrounded the unfinished pyramid and grew with it. However, none of these interpretations was agreed upon by the scholars. The most fascinating

Transporting a block of stone, bas-relief from Maasara, Egyptian Museum, Cairo.

Scenes such as this suggest the enormous effort that was required to build the pyramids.

proposals come, once again, from the writings of ancient Greek and Roman historians which mentioned 'terraces' (Diodorus Siculus) and 'hills' (Pliny), made of salt and nitre, that surrounded the pyramids like embankments that increased in width and height, but always with a very gentle slope, as the pyramid grew taller. At the conclusion of the work, these earthworks would have been dissolved by deviating the course of the Nile, thus creating an artificial flood. Egyptologists seem more inclined to accept the idea that ramps were used, but there is no consensus about what type of structures these would have been. Some sustain that the ramps to transport the blocks would have been simple, straight platforms placed on one side of the pyramids that became narrower and longer as the construction proceeded. Others are inclined to believe that spiral ramps surrounded the mass of the pyramid and

went up as the pyramid rose. According to yet another theory, there were many small ramps all around the construction of the pyramid, substituted at the final stages of the work by a single straight ramp on one side.

As for the material used to built the ramps, a likely possibility would be palm trunks and unbaked mud bricks, but this too is only a hypothesis. On the contrary, one aspect that is known for certain, because it is documented by the bas-reliefs in the tombs, is that the blocks of stone were pulled up the ramps using wooden sleds, lubricated with a mixture of water and silt to improve gliding and reduce weight.

Another unanswered question related to the ramps is about their fate: were they demolished at the end of construction? Or were they dismantled, using another army of men for all the time that was needed, considering their colossal dimensions? According to some scholars, such structures were conserved and re-used to create the ceremonial roads that connected the principal buildings of the funeral complexes. The most recent theory in this field was developed by a French architect, Pierre Crozat, who theorizes that the pyramids were built by accretion, starting from a central nucleus to which the other blocks were added. At the beginning there would have been no need for ramps used only to raise the largest blocks. Later the ramps would have been absorbed into the construction itself, thus eliminating the burden of having to demolish them. While we still don't know if it took 20 years and thousands of workers to build a pyramid, we can safely affirm that centuries of study have not been sufficient to reveal the pyramids' secrets.

Pyramid of Khafre with the tomb of the dignitary Seshemnefer in the foreground, Giza.

After all these centuries, it is still not clear how these architectural masterpieces were built.

View of the
pyramids on
the Giza plateau.
The symbol of
Egypt at the time
of the pharaohs,
the pyramids
continue to
fascinate
visitors and to
inspire heated
discussions.

THE REMAINS OF A CIVILIZATION
THE OLD KINGDOM: THE AGE
OF THE GREAT PYRAMIDS

Head of a falcon, gold and obsidian, from Nekhen (Hieraconpolis), c. 2200 BC, Egyptian Museum, Cairo. The falcon was the totem animal of Horus, the god identified with the pharaoh himself.

During the Old Kingdom, thanks to the guidance of Pharaoh Djoser (Zoser) and the exceptional capability of his architect Imhotep, the pyramids were born, the immortal monuments of a thousand-year civilization that expressed an unwavering aspiration toward the divine in all its artistic undertakings.

Metaphors of an ideology in which this great religious fervour was united with concrete political requirements, the pyramids have conserved their enormous power of fascination through the centuries, further exalted by the complex series of buildings and monuments that surround them. Nothing seems to have been left to chance: each element contributed to the eternal glory of the pharaoh, the supreme representative of a civilization that also benefited eternally from the eternal blessedness of its leader.

THE DAWN OF EGYPTIAN CIVILIZATION

In the mid-4ᵗʰ millennium BC
Egypt was divided into two
kingdoms: Upper Egypt in
the south, with its capital
at Nekhen (Hieraconpolis),
where the principal gods
to be venerated were Seth,
embodied by the pharaoh
wearing a red crown, and the
cobra goddess Wadjet; and
the north or Lower Egypt,
which placed itself under
the protection of the vulture
goddess Nekhbet, had its

most important city at Behdet.
Here the pharaoh wore a white
crown and was considered a
direct descendent of the falcon
god Horus, the protector of
the kingdom.

The history of this period
is rather controversial. It
is known that, at first, the
northern kingdom prevailed
over the southern in battle and
extended its power over Upper
Egypt. During this period the
cult of Ra, the sun god of

Sources for the Reconstruction of Egyptian Chronology

The exact historical chronology of the ancient Egyptian peoples is still the object of heated debate among scholars. Fortunately, its reconstruction has been made possible by the discovery of an important series of papyrus scrolls and engravings that include the so-called royal lists, that list of the pharaohs' names in the order of their reigns. Among these documents, the most important are the *Table of Abydos*, a funeral relief from the period of the New Kingdom engraved on the walls of the temple of Seti I (father of the famous Ramesses II), which depicts the pharaoh while he renders homage to 76 ancestors, and the *Palermo stone*, a black basalt commemorative plaque or *stele* from the Old Kingdom period, engraved on both sides with the names of the pharaohs, the names of their mothers and the number of years each reigned.

In addition to this group of sources, much additional information has been provided by historians who lived long after the events they narrate. The most famous of these is Manetho, an Egyptian priest who lived during the 3rd century BC on the Nile Delta, who wrote his book *Aegyptiaca* in Greek. In this book the author told the history of his country, and included a list of all the kings who had reigned, divided into 30 dynasties. Unfortunately his work has survived only in fragments and in summaries written by later authors such as Josephus, historian of the 1st and 2nd centuries AD, and Eusebius, a Christian annalist who lived during the 4th century. Despite various lacunae, Manetho's list is the most commonly used basis for dating the principal events of Egyptian history.

The dynasties of the Old Kingdom and the principal pharaohs

Protodynastic period	3000–2686 BC	
1st Dynasty	3000-2890 BC	
2nd Dynasty	2890-2686 BC	
Old Kingdom	2686-2160 BC	
3rd Dynasty	2686-2613 BC	Djoser (Zoser)
		Huni
4th Dynasty	2613-2494 BC	Sneferu
		Khufu (Cheops)
		Djedefra (Radjedef)
		Khafre (Chephren)
		Menkaura (Mycerinus)
		Shepseskaf
5th Dynasty	2494-2345 AC	Userkaf
		Sahure
		Nyuserre Ini
		Djedkare Isesi
		Unas
6th Dynasty	2345-2181 BC	Teti
		Pepi I
		Merenre Nemtyemsaf I
		Pepi II
7th-8th Dynasties	2181-2160 BC	

Heliopolis, spread throughout the territory of Egypt. This deity became fundamentally important to the history of the monarchy because, according to the religious creed that was developed to legitimate the absolute power of the pharaoh, the ruler was believed to be the son of Ra, born of the union of the god with the queen mother.

The activities of the populations of the north and the south were rather basic consisting primarily of agriculture and the production of ceramics, linen and stone tools.

Archaeological finds from the settlements of this period demonstrate, however, that the bases for a hierarchical society had already been laid, and that it would evolve during the intermediate phase of the Protodynastic period to reach full maturity during the Old Kingdom.

The god Horus portrayed as a falcon, 304-330 BC, Edfu. Horus was the principal god of Lower Egypt.

The Narmer
Tablet, front
(right) and
back (opposite)
from Nekhen
(Hieraconpolis),
c. 3000 BC,
Egyptian
Museum, Cairo.
According to
tradition, it was
Narmer who
achieved the
unification of
the two regions,
Upper and
Lower Egypt.

The Unification of the Two Kingdoms

A short time after the victory of the north, revolts once again split the nation and led to a conflict that, at the beginning of the 3rd millennium BC, definitively overturned the situation. It led to stable control by the kingdom of the south, and the union of Upper and Lower Egypt. According to tradition, this union took place under Pharaoh Narmer, according to the evidence of the tablet found at Hierankonpolis, where he is shown in the act of conquering and vanquishing his enemies. This pharaoh is credited with the foundation of the capital of the unified kingdom, Memphis, built symbolically at the point where the delta meets the Nile valley.

The separate identities of the two parts of the nation were however named and celebrated in the royal titles and in the rituals of the jubilee festival. A highly symbolic double crown was used during

The Titles of the Pharaohs and Symbols of Power

The word 'pharaoh' is a Greek version of an Egyptian word, *per-aa*, originally used to indicate the royal residence; only after the second half of the 9th century BC did it accompany the name of the ruler. A series of titles indicated the characteristics and prerogatives of the king: the pharaoh bore the names of Horus, the falcon god venerated in Upper Egypt and whom he incarnated, of the cobra goddess Wadjet, of the vulture goddess Nekhbet of Lower Egypt, and on the hieroglyphic cartouches of many monuments he was also entitled the 'son of Ra'.

The divine nature of the king was also expressed in the stereotyped forms of representation: the figure of the pharaoh is always larger than his subjects, he wears the crown of Upper or Lower Egypt (sometimes both united together), his head is adorned by the *uraeus* (the cobra that represented the goddess Wadjet and the power of the king); other symbols that identified the pharaoh are the bull's tail and the artificial beard.

the coronation of the pharaoh: the white part represented the king's authority over the southern kingdom, the red crown represented the submission of the northern kingdom. This reference to the double kingdom was also present in the jubilee ritual (*Heb-Sed*), the most important celebration of ancient Egypt, during which the pharaoh kindled the energy to combat the forces of evil and to maintain the stability of his reign through a symbolic series of rituals. The ceremony was long and complex. A procession led by the pharaoh and the statues of the gods reached the site of four pavilions. Once inside, the pharaoh was again invested as king of Upper and Lower

Egypt. In the evening, holding a symbol of his sovereignty over the two kingdoms, he ran a short distance in a ritual demonstration of his renewed strength. The unification of the two kingdoms was therefore personified by the figure of the pharaoh, although the separatist tendency was always present in the history of Egypt and reappeared forcefully at the times of the greatest crises. Religion played an essential role in stabilizing the situation. It was said that the sovereigns of the first two dynasties were entitled to reign because they descended directly from the gods, and therefore they guaranteed the welfare, the justice and the serenity of the Egyptian people on Earth.

Calcite vase with relief decorations depicting the jubilee rite of *Heb-Sed*, from the funerary complex of Djoser at Saqqara, c. 2700 BC,

Egyptian Museum, Cairo. During the celebration of *Heb-Sed*, the ritual that sanctified the union of the two kingdoms was repeated.

Two statues
of Ranefer,
high priest
of Memphis,
with different
clothing
and hair
arrangements,
c. 2470 BC,
from Saqqara,
Egyptian
Museum,
Cairo. The high
priest and the
vizier occupied
the highest
ranks after the
pharaoh.

Politics and Society in the Old Kingdom

Woman using a grindstone, statuette from Saqqara, 5th dynasty (2494-2345 BC), Egyptian Museum, Cairo. Slaves and workers who did menial tasks were at the bottom of the Egyptian social hierarchy.

Egyptian society was a hierarchy, with the pharaoh and his family at the top. They were followed by high dignitaries, such as the vizier, the high priests of the various cults and high officials of the army. The next level included scribes, priests, soldiers, artisans and specialized workers, and finally, at the bottom, were farmers and slaves.

The numerous host of royal dignitaries, whether relatives of the king or simply citizens whose honesty and loyalty had distinguished them, were nominated by the pharaoh himself. They held office for life and they were paid handsomely to ensure that dissatisfaction would not endanger the kingdom.

The most important office was that of the vizier, who acted as the chief of justice, chief architect and also custodian of the archives. Such a dignitary was often believed to possess special magical and religious powers, as in the case of Imhotep, vizier during the reign of Pharaoh Djoser, who became an object of a popular cult because he was considered to be a great healer.

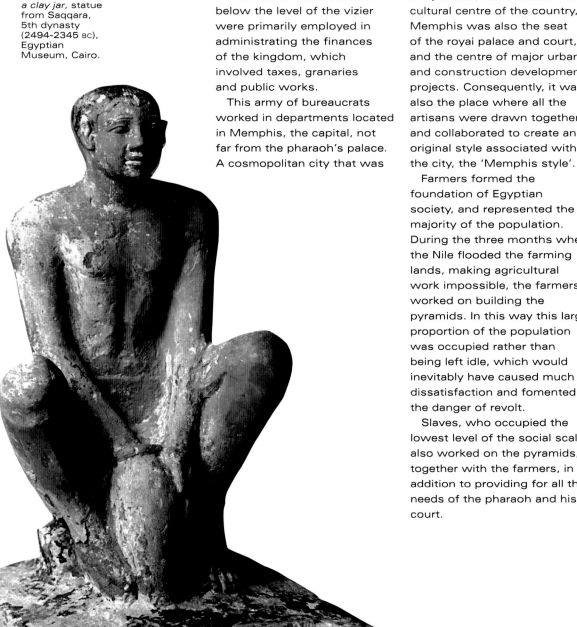

Artisan finishing a clay jar, statue from Saqqara, 5th dynasty (2494-2345 BC), Egyptian Museum, Cairo.

Most of the other officials below the level of the vizier were primarily employed in administrating the finances of the kingdom, which involved taxes, granaries and public works.

This army of bureaucrats worked in departments located in Memphis, the capital, not far from the pharaoh's palace. A cosmopolitan city that was the political, administrative and cultural centre of the country, Memphis was also the seat of the royal palace and court, and the centre of major urban and construction development projects. Consequently, it was also the place where all the artisans were drawn together and collaborated to create an original style associated with the city, the 'Memphis style'.

Farmers formed the foundation of Egyptian society, and represented the majority of the population. During the three months when the Nile flooded the farming lands, making agricultural work impossible, the farmers worked on building the pyramids. In this way this large proportion of the population was occupied rather than being left idle, which would inevitably have caused much dissatisfaction and fomented the danger of revolt.

Slaves, who occupied the lowest level of the social scale, also worked on the pyramids, together with the farmers, in addition to providing for all the needs of the pharaoh and his court.

Woman making beer, statuette from Giza, c. 2300 BC, Egyptian Museum, Cairo.

Farmer ploughing, painted wooden model, Louvre, Paris. When they were not busy in the fields, farmers were called on to work on construction of the pyramids.

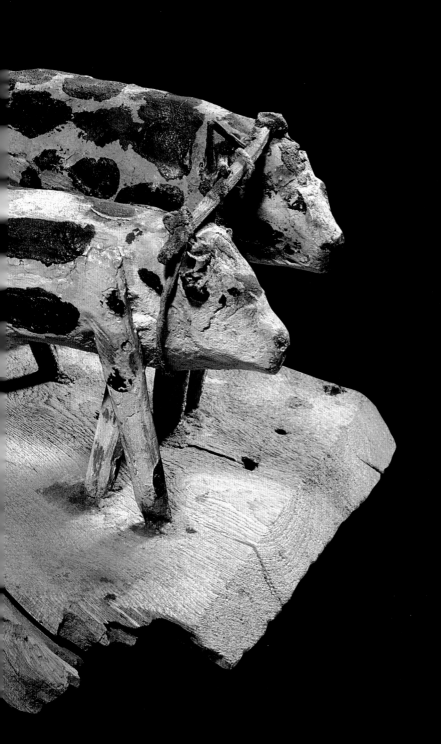

Priest Ka-aper, wooden statue from Saqqara, c. 2450 BC, Egyptian Museum, Cairo. The priestly class retained an important role throughout the history of ancient Egypt.

Priests of Heliopolis and the Great Ennead

From a religious point of view, the new unified kingdom appeared to be a rather chaotic collection of doctrines and cults of different sorts. Each of the cities venerated its own gods: this lack of cohesion could have become a serious problem for a country governed by a monarchy whose absolute power was derived from religion. The various priestly orders were therefore encouraged by the central powers to reorder this chaos, to revise the doctrines of the individual cities and unify them in a single religious creed. The priests of Heliopolis, the ancient city of On, not far from modern Cairo, played the leading role in this effort. They developed the great Ennead doctrine (the group of nine deities) that was based, first of all, on a synthesis of the sun-god doctrine of Ra with that of Osiris, through a series of compromises and adjustments of the various myths of the origins of the universe.

A first solution to this delicate operation was adopted at the beginning of the 3rd Dynasty, but was not definitively resolved until the 4th Dynasty, the dynasty of the Giza pyramids, when the doctrine exalted a monarchy based on the sun, and thus was linked to Ra, but also maintained the importance of the cult of Horus. According to the doctrine developed by the priests of Heliopolis, the first action of the first god, Atum, was to create light, or Ra, who was identified as Ra-Atum. He then generated, again on his own through spit or masturbating sperm, the first divine couple of Shu, the male who personified the atmosphere, and Tefnut, the female who personified water. From their union, Geb, the god of the earth, and Nut, the goddess of the sky, were born and they in turn generated four non-cosmic deities: Osiris, Isis, Set e Nephthys. Horus, the son of Isis and Osiris, was chosen by the assembly of the gods to govern; their decision was guaranteed by Geb and announced by Ra. The new cosmogony had succeeded in bringing together and unifying the diverse beliefs of the kingdom, to create a religious creed that was focused on the central figure of the pharaoh, considered a direct descendant of the gods and their intermediary on the earth. The absolute powers of the king were therefore, justified and guaranteed directly by their divine origin. In this way an essential bond between religion and the state was fashioned that would be the basis of the whole history of Egypt. The most important concern of the whole population was the wellbeing of the pharaoh, his earthly needs and, above all, the cultivation of his goodwill after death, so that he would watch over them forever. This last aspect was by far the most important, in the conviction that preserving the

Osiris, statue from Saqqara, c. 530 BC, Egyptian Museum, Cairo. Osiris was one of the most important divinities in the new doctrine codified by the priests of Heliopolis.

earthly remains of the king
and celebrating daily rites
would serve to guarantee
wellbeing and serenity to
the whole community. In
this context, architecture
played a fundamental role:
it was conceived as an
instrument of providing for
the eternal requirements of
the sovereign and, at the
same time, to represent
the sovereign himself. The
progression, through a series
of intermediate steps, from
simple structures such as
the mastaba tombs to very
elaborate buildings such as the
pyramids of Giza, is therefore
closely linked to a complex
series of historical, political
and religious transformations.

*Isis nursing
Horus*, statue,
c. 1st-3rd
century AD,
Museo
Gregoriano
Egizio, Vatican
Palaces, Rome.
According to
the Egyptian
religion, Isis
was both sister
and wife of
Osiris.

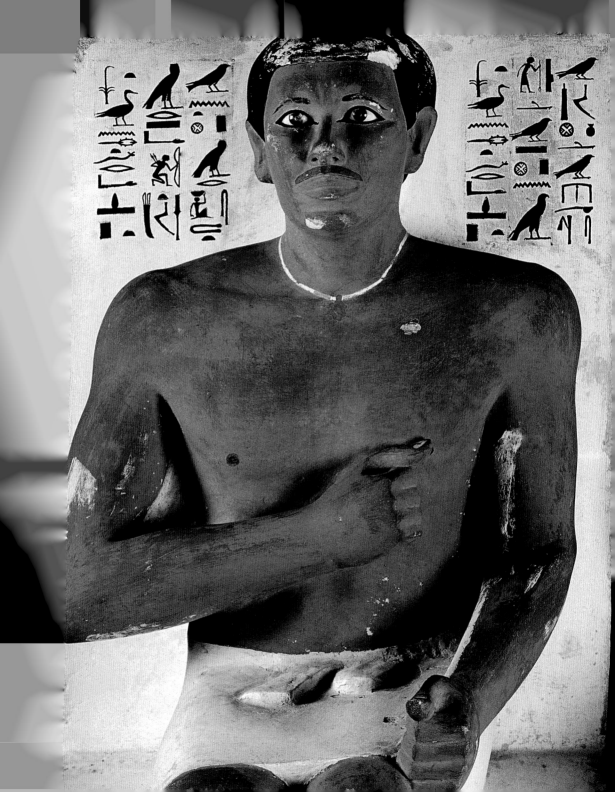

Before the Pyramids: the Mastaba

Scenes of papyrus harvesting, pasture and hunting, polychrome relief, c. 2450 BC, mastaba of Nefer and Ka-hay, Saqqara.

The lavish decorations of these monuments confirm that they were made for people who had particularly important status in Egyptian society.

The kings of the Protodynastic period adopted a new type of tomb, the mastaba, which became very popular in the Egyptian world. The mastaba was an architectural structure which came to replace traditional burials in excavated graves for high-ranking individuals. The typical Protodynastic mastaba developed from a simpler structure of the Predynastic period, which included several partially buried chambers where the corpse was deposited after being wrapped in mats, later substituted by coffins that were deposited in cavities between the floor and the walls. The evolution of this type of structure led to the development of real buildings, similar to the houses that the deceased had inhabited during their lives, but endowed with the special purpose of serving as dwellings for eternity. At the beginning the occupants of the tombs were kings, but when pyramids became the tombs of the pharaohs, beginning with the step pyramid of King Djoser, the mastabas continued to be used for the burial of other important personages such as the relatives of the pharaoh and members of court.

The term *mastaba*, which means bench, referring to the masonry benches that stand in front of Arab dwellings, has

Entrance to
the mastaba
of Mereruka,
c. 2330 BC,
Saqqara.
The mastaba
substituted

earlier rock-cut
tombs, and
became the
typical tomb
for pharaohs
before the
pyramids.

been adopted by Egyptologists to indicate a simple tomb composed of two parts: one was partially sunken and served as the burial chamber; the other part, at ground level, was built of stone or unbaked brick and was composed of several chambers that, in addition to containing all the fittings for the deceased, also served as a shrine. The exterior was decorated with mouldings to imitate the facades of palaces. Conceptually, the organization of the mastabas was quite similar to that of the pyramids. For example, they both had boundary walls outside of which there were some auxiliary burials, identified without a doubt as those of servants. Slaves were, in fact, poisoned to death when their masters died, or else were buried alive.

At the end of the 18th century a group of 16 tombs was excavated in the necropolis of Abydos, a site in Upper Egypt near Thinis, the birthplace and burial site of the kings of the Thinnite Dynasty. After getting started in the worst possible way,

with the destruction of much material and the loss of valuable data, the work went forward under the direction of archaeologist William Matthew Flinders Petrie. He collected much clearer data about the mastabas of Abydos. These followed the traditional structure of being partly underground and partly at ground level, marked in this case by a mound of sand. At Saqqara the sites explored by William Emery revealed, on the other hand, a series of mastabas with ground level structures that imitated palace facades: these were larger, and had more orderly arrangements of the underground chambers than the tombs at Abydos. The differences between the two necropoli are structural because, presumably, the rituals were similar in the two locations. The two groups of royal tombs indicate that the kings of the 1st Dynasty habitually built two tombs for themselves: an empty, symbolic tomb at Abydos, the true tomb at Saqqara. The existence of the two burial grounds is definitely proven,

Opposite: *Portrait of Nefer*, the occupant of the tomb, polychrome relief, c. 2450 BC, mastaba of Nefer and Ka-hay, Saqqara.

After pyramids became the typical funerary monument for the pharaoh, mastabas were retained for his family members and important court dignitaries

but it seems probable that the two necropoli symbolized the double role of the kings as sovereigns of Upper and Lower Egypt, a custom that was perpetuated by the later dynasties. The royal mastabas, soon supplanted by pyramids, did not last as long as the mastabas for other high-ranking citizens. All around the pyramids on the Giza plain there are countless buildings of this type, set out in a very orderly way around the tombs of the pharaohs. The upper part of the structure, intended to be a shrine for the cult of the deceased, was the most developed part of the tomb from the 4th Dynasty onwards. The numerous chambers were decorated with coloured bas-reliefs depicting all sorts of subjects and situations such as deposition of offerings for the deceased, scenes of country life and scenes of hunting and fishing. The deceased is normally depicted in these scenes as the supervisor of the activities, in the company of his wife. In the main room, where the most important ceremonies were held, the greatest attention was focused on the decoration of the false door. This had sculpted jambs and an architrave like a real doorway. The *stele* or commemorative plaques that stood in front of the altar, oriented to the west, were believed to enable the deceased to move back and forth between the world of the dead and the living at his pleasure.

Opposite:
Bas-relief showing several scribes, c. 2330 BC, mastaba of Mereruka, Saqqara.

Following pages:
Bas-relief, from the mastaba of Ipy at Saqqara, Sixth dynasty (2345–2181 BC), Egyptian Museum, Cairo.

FROM THE CONCEPT OF THE MASTABA TO THE PYRAMID

The Egyptians attached great importance to the appearance of their tombs and the links to their political and religious beliefs. Djoser's choice to pass from the mastaba to the step pyramid must have been full of these implications.

The royal tomb became an essential instrument to permit the pharaoh to make his voyage to afterlife; this concept was defined toward the end of the 2nd Dynasty.

The mastaba remained in use for high-ranking personages. It was still a very respectable type of residence, but not sufficiently developed for a complex solar cult such as that being developed at the end of the Protodynastic period.

In this belief system, the king sat after death at the side of his father Ra, and continued to offer his protection to his subjects, as long as they honoured his memory with daily rituals.

The pyramids, together with the wider funeral complex of which they were the central focus, served to guarantee the performance of these rites, and also to preserve the king's body from harm for eternity.

Naturally, a civilization so dedicated to symbolism would not have chosen the form of its most important monuments in a casual way: the king's tomb had to indicate the tie with divinity very clearly.

The first structures emphasized, through vertical elements, the extension of the pharaoh toward the divine.

Beginning with what was already familiar, that is the mastaba, under King Djoser a new type of tomb was created by piling up several mastabas of decreasing dimensions, to symbolize a giant staircase for the spirit of the pharaoh to climb to the heavens.

Later the pharaoh's tombs took on the form of the Giza

Previous pages:
Scenes of pasture and fishing, polychrome relief, c. 2450 BC, mastaba of Nefer and Ka-hay, Saqqara.

Opposite: Interior of the mastaba of Mereruka, a government official, c. 2323 BC, Saqqara. Statue of the pharaoh in a niche on the back wall, with an offering table at his feet.

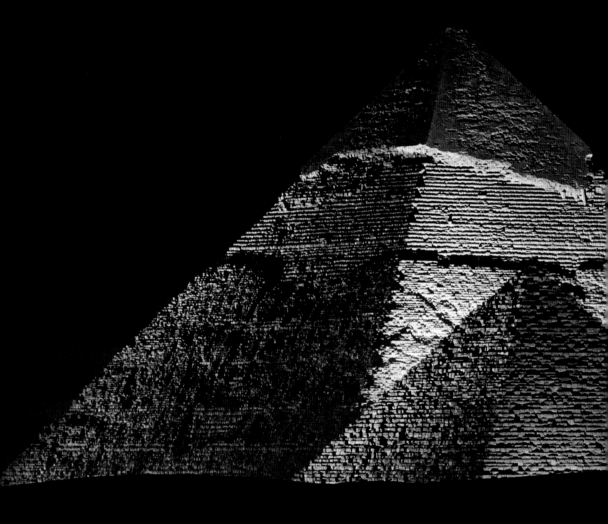

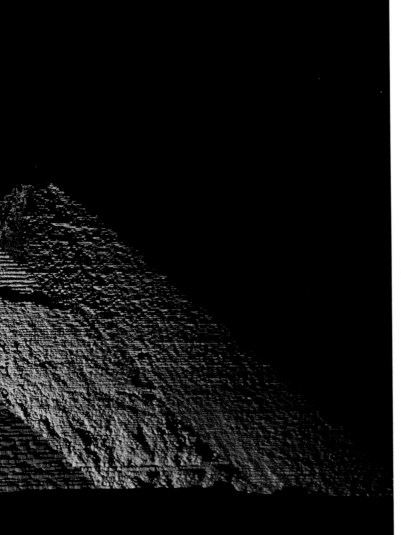

pyramids. The three axes of
the pyramids represented
significant concepts: the
vertical axis represented the
aspiration to the divine that
linked the pharaoh to his
father Ra; the north-south
axis was the earthly axis,
parallel to the Nile that was
so important for the Egyptian
people; the east-west axis,
which indicated the path
of the sun, represented the
heavens, and its daily cycle
of death and resurrection
was a symbol of constant
regeneration.

View of
the pyramids
of Giza,
c. 2570-2520 BC.
They represent
the next step
of evolution
after the step
pyramids.

The Organization of the Tomb Complex

Walls, Djoser's funerary complex, c. 2650 BC, Saqqara. The complex is composed of the step pyramid and several buildings for funeral rites and cult of the deceased pharaoh.

The majesty of the pyramids has always attracted the attention of all those who stop to admire them. However, it is mistaken to consider only

their geometric perfection as isolated structures. They were each, in fact, at the heart of a great and highly developed tomb complex with important cultural and ritual functions that first appeared with King Djoser, and was developed and refined to take on its definitive form under Sneferu, first king of the 4th Dynasty. The complex was composed of a group of buildings arranged along a precise route, also charged with ritual and liturgical significance. There was a very long ceremonial access avenue, marked by walls, and later covered over, that led from the lower temple, along the banks of the Nile or on a canal connected to the river, to the funerary temple located to the east of the pyramid. The funerary temple was originally a simple chapel, but was soon transformed into a more complex structure of several chambers. The pyramids of the queens and other family members were distributed around the

View of the pyramid of Khufu, with two satellite pyramids in the foreground, Giza.

The smaller monuments may have been made for the queens or relatives of the pharaoh.

complex, in numbers that vary from site to site. The pyramid and the funerary temple were protected by an enclosure: in the older complexes this was a single wall, while the more recent had double walls. Another wall surrounded this kernel and the other annexes of the pyramid. Often the secondary elements of the complex, such as the queens' pyramids, the ceremonial avenue and the valley temple, were situated between the inner and outer enclosures.

Interior of
the tomb of
Meresankh, one
of Khafre's wives,
c. 2540 BC, Giza.

Colonnade,
Djoser's
funerary
complex,
c. 2650 BC,
Saqqara.
This complex
represents
the architect
Imhotep's
masterpiece.

The oldest stone building in Egypt is the step pyramid of Djoser, made for the king of the 3rd Dynasty who was buried in a crypt at the bottom of a pit underneath the structure. Djoser began construction of his tomb shortly after his coronation. The designer of this extraordinary monument was Imhotep the architect, the first in history to use dressed stone for the construction of a large structure, in addition to being one of the few architects whose name was immortalized by the Egyptians.

The building, which represented the first step of evolution of the pyramid toward the geometric form at Giza, still towers over the ancient necropolis of Saqqara. It is in an excellent state of repair, with the exception of the very top, where some stones were carried away in ancient times to be re-used elsewhere.

The original structure of the mastaba was, in this project, amplified to six steps of decreasing dimensions, while the underground space was extended into a series of chambers that served as storerooms and burial chambers, connected by a series of corridors. In the royal chamber the walls were lavishly decorated with mosaics of stone and glazed terracotta. Here two alabaster sarcophagi were found: one intended for a queen; the other containing a wooden coffin with the skeleton of a child and two vases covered with gold leaf and cornelian beads. The chambers that served as storerooms were full of vases that were originally stacked up to the ceiling. They were shattered when the ceiling collapsed. The total number of vases was about 40,000, all made of stone such as alabaster or porphyry. The step pyramid was the focus

Imhotep, statuette detail, c. 600-501 BC, Science Museum, London.

Imhotep, the Genial Architect

The emergence of important families at court began during the reign of Djoser. Imhotep was undoubtedly one of the most important personages, and his fame was very long lasting. His name and his titles have been conserved in an inscription on the base of a statue of Djoser, where he was called the Royal Seal-Bearer and the High Priest of Ptah. He was responsible for the construction of the first step pyramid, which was a completely new kind of architecture. The architect used dressed stone blocks for the interior and the exterior of the buildings. These blocks were not much larger that the unbaked bricks that were normally employed, but it was the first time the new material was used; however it was not until the period of the Giza pyramids that stone would have become the customary material.

Imhotep was so greatly appreciated that during the 26th Dynasty (664-525 BC), he was deified as a Son of Ptah and invoked as the protector of the poor and the sick.

of a funerary complex in an enclosure that measured approximately 550 x 278 metres, oriented along a north-south axis. It included four independent parts: in addition to the pyramid, there were also the south tomb, the jubilee court and the funerary temple, each with its own annexes. The boundary wall was made of white limestone and was

probably intended to reproduce the appearance of the walls around Djoser's palace.

The other constructions, all in pairs, also reproduced existing structures of the king's palace, confirming that the whole complex was considered a residence for the afterlife. Inside these buildings the ceremonies were prepared and then carried out

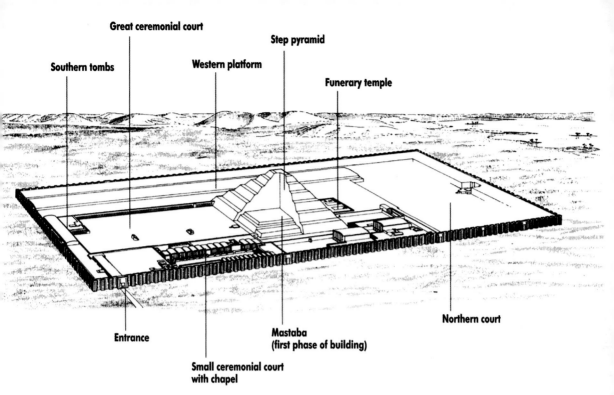

Great ceremonial court

Step pyramid

Southern tombs

Western platform

Funerary temple

Entrance

**Mastaba
(first phase of building)**

Northern court

**Small ceremonial court
with chapel**

Opposite:
Stone jars,
from Djoser's
step pyramid
at Saqqara,
c. 3000-2700 BC,
Egyptian
Museum, Cairo.
The funerary
complex
was used to
celebrate rituals
and make
offerings to
the deceased
pharaoh.

Reconstruction
of Djoser's
funerary
complex (from
R. Schulz, M.
Seidel, *Egypt*,
Cologne 1998,
p. 48, fig. 9).

at the same time in the two
twin buildings, out of respect
for the duality of Upper and
Lower Egypt. One of the most
important of the ceremonies
was the coronation of the
pharaoh after death, which
was repeated at regular
intervals. It seems that in the
distant past the king on the
throne was actually killed, in
a ritual of human sacrifice,
to be replaced by another,
younger ruler, to guarantee the
prosperity of the kingdom. In
Djoser's time, human sacrifice

was no longer practiced. The
propitiatory function of the
sacrifice had been substituted
by magic formulas. The vitality
of the king after death was
also confirmed by the presence
of a small chamber, open to
the living, where offerings of
food were left for the dead,
under the surveillance of a
statue that personified the king
and, according to the religious
beliefs of the time, controlled
the correct performance of
the rites. The design of this
funerary complex remained

Offering Tables

Offering tables were normally used during the ceremonies in honour of the deceased, to offer sacrifices to the gods. Two objects of this type come from a royal funerary complex that had been destroyed during the construction of Djoser's step pyramid. The identical and wonderfully elaborate tables presumably date to the end of the 2nd Dynasty or the early years of Djoser's reign. Two marvellously sculpted and majestic lions emerge from the rectangular block of alabaster that forms the structure. The heads of the animals are raised and encircled by their manes, the front paws are sculpted in high relief, while the tails are wrapped around the shallow basin that was intended to collect the liquids of the offerings. The lion motif is well documented in Egyptian iconography where, as a symbol of force, power and pride, it was used to represent the pharaoh himself.

Detail from the panel of green and blue glazed ceramic from the funerary complex of Djoser at Saqqara, c. 2650 BC, Egyptian Museum, Cairo. The panel imitated the mats that hung on the walls of the royal palaces.

an isolated project. The exact circumstances that underlay its creation remain unknown. It is known, however, that it was here, thanks to the work of Imhotep, that wooden architecture gave way to stone architecture on a monumental scale. The new stone architecture adapted most of its structural elements from the wood. For example, the wooden posts that sustained the roofs became elegant, fluted columns of stone, and the glazed tiles imitated the mats that hung outside the palaces.

Offering table,
from the
funerary
complex
of Djoser
at Saqqara,
c. 2650 BC,
Egyptian
Museum, Cairo.
Offerings were
made to the
gods during
the ceremonies
in honour
of the dead.

Transformation into the Geometric Pyramid: Huni and Sneferu

The end of the 3rd Dynasty marked a change in the architecture of the funerary complexes. This change began under the last king of this dynasty, Huni, and was carried forward by his son Sneferu. Huni had a step pyramid, similar to that of Djoser, built at Meidum.

Today it is hard to see because it collapsed in part after Arab despoilers, during the Middle Ages, carried off the highest blocks by rolling them down.

The initial project was subjected to more than one variation during the course of construction. It was intended to be a seven-level structure and was later enlarged.

However it is almost certain that Huni never used it, because his son Sneferu adopted it as his eternal abode.

During the reign of Sneferu, the stepped structure was transformed into a regular pyramid, by filling in the steps with blocks of stone. This was the birth of the first geometric pyramid, 91.9 metres high and 144 metres along each baseline, with an inclination of about 50 degrees. This pharaoh had three pyramids built, the last of which, the so-called red pyramid, was designed and built according to the principles of the real geometric pyramids.

Sneferu was also the author of important changes in the organization of the accompanying funerary complex, which marked a turning point in the evolution toward the structures of the Giza plain.

Sneferu introduced a second temple, the valley temple, in addition to the funerary temple as adopted by Djoser.

Pyramid of Sneferu, c. 2590 BC, Meidum. This represents the intermediate phase between the step pyramid at Saqqara and the Giza pyramids.

What does the Word Pyramid Mean?

The word pyramid is of Greek origin and derives from *pyramis*, the name of a sweet made of grain, made typically in a conical form. It was offered by Greek mercenaries for their dead companions. The Egyptians called the pyramids *mer*, a word that can be translated as 'the site of ascension', evidently alluding to the function of the pyramid as a mean for the sovereigns to reach the heavens and join their father, the god Ra. In the texts about the pyramids, written in buildings erected after the period of the Old Kingdom, they are mentioned as the kings' stairways to the heavens. The appearance of these monuments, completely covered with white limestone, could have been an attempt to symbolize a ray of sunlight that would carry the ruler to the heavens or bring him down to his earthly sepulchre to take possession of the tributes of food that were left for him after death.

During this phase of great innovations, the discovery of the infinite solutions that the use of stone as a building material could offer was fundamental.

During Djoser's time, the architectural creations used stone simply to transpose schemes already used in building with wood. Later, as mastery of the material grew, stone was used to create funerary complexes composed of majestic buildings.

Northern or red pyramid of Sneferu, c. 2590 BC, Dahshur. This is the third pyramid built by Sneferu and represents a prelude to the successive geometric pyramids of Giza.

The 'bent'
pyramid
of Sneferu,
c. 2600 BC,
Dahshur.
The funerary
buildings of
this pharaoh
developed
from Djoser's
complex.

The Ritual Pyramids

The ritual or satellite pyramids are built next to the major pyramids and are complete replicas of them, except on a smaller scale. Scholars do not agree completely about their function. The idea that they were used as tombs for the queens has been rejected because the pyramids of the queens are also accompanied by a tiny ritual pyramid. It seems just as unlikely that they were actually tombs, because it would not have been possible to move coffins and sarcophagi through the narrow corridors that lead to the internal chambers. Furthermore, there are no signs of decorations or finishing on the walls. On the basis of these facts, associated with the finding of containers for offerings, some scholars consider that these were places for offerings to Ra, in exchange for which the worshippers requested the wellbeing of the deceased in the after world.

Alternatively, it has been proposed that these were ritual structures created for the *ka* of the king, that is the personification of the life force, guide and protector, the true essence of the individual.

THE SEVENTH WONDER: THE GIZA PYRAMIDS

Towering over the Giza Plain, the three differently sized pyramids of the descendants of Sneferu have fascinated generations of scholars and enthusiasts for centuries. The gigantic proportions of these extraordinary monuments are most striking. The blocks of local limestone that were used have been estimated to weigh up to 220 tonnes each! The term Giza, in Arabic, refers to a limestone plateau. The area of the site is not very extensive: it was defined by two streams that have dried up, and it slopes gently down to the Nile. During the 4th Dynasty, impressive earthworks created the surface for construction, one after another, of the three pyramids, and it seems that some of the blocks came from the margins of the plateau itself. The limited area of the site was completely exploited by the three kings who built their tombs here, accompanied by an seemingly unending series of mastabas for all the court dignitaries who had the honour to be buried near to their ruler. These funeral complexes were designed to create surroundings worthy of the majesty of the pyramids. The complex of Khafre alone, for example, must have contained over a hundred statues of the sovereign. The pyramids of Khufu, Khafre and Menkaura, with their subsidiary structures, occupied almost the whole surface available for building on the Giza Plain. Their descendants were therefore forced to move elsewhere to build their tombs.

Aerial view
of the Giza
pyramids.

An Unflattering Portrait

Very few sources of information are available about the life and reign of Khufu. Among these are the rather bitter comments left by the Greek historian Herodotus, who described the pharaoh as follows: 'They said that [...] while Khufu reigned over them [the Egyptian people], he reduced them to extreme misery. In fact, after he had closed all the temples, first he prohibited sacrifices, then he commanded all of the Egyptians to work for him [...]. And one hundred thousand men worked at a time, continuously, each group for three months. So the people passed ten years of hardships to build the road where they dragged the stones [...]. For the pyramid itself they say another twenty years went by until it was built [...]. They also say that Khufu became so wicked that, when he needed money he put his daughter into a brothel and ordered her to demand a certain amount of money, though they didn't say exactly how much. She obeyed the orders of her father and also wanted to leave her own monument and asked each man who lay with her to give her a stone. And they said that with these stones the pyramid in the middle of the three in front of the Great Pyramid was built'. (History, II, 124-127)

Build a Stairway to Heaven... and He Will Climb it...

The Great Pyramid of Khufu was the first to be built on the Giza Plain: it is the one that attracts the greatest attention from scholars and fascinates the enthusiasts. Every sort of theory has been suggested to explain this monument. From the myriad of mysteries that surround it, the strangest beliefs have sprung up, including those about its alleged magical powers. The structure's essential statistics are mind-boggling. It has been calculated, for example, that the perimeter of its base could contain the Florence and Milan cathedrals and the basilica of Saint Peter's in Rome all together. Napoleon amused himself by estimating that, with the stones of the pyramids, he could have built a wall three metres high and thirty centimetres thick around the borders of France. The monument, built during the reign of Khufu (2589–2566 BC), is really magnificent: the base measures 230.40 x 230.51 x 230.60 x 230.54 metres, with a difference of only 11-20 centimetres along the four sides. Originally it was 14.670 metres high, but today the top point, the so-called *pyramidion* is missing, so it measures 137.25 metres to the top. It is built of 2,300,000 blocks, each weighing an average of 2.5 tonnes, for a total weight of 6,500,000 tonnes.

The inclination is 51.52 degrees. The main entrance is on the north facade, a monumental entrance that leads, through a passageway, to a chamber that has no apparent function. Another corridor leads upward to another chamber, perfectly centred on the vertical axis of the pyramid. This is called the 'Queen's chamber' by modern scholars, although it is

Opposite: Khufu, statuette in ivory from Abydos, c. 2570 BC, Egyptian Museum, Cairo. The most important and universally recognized legacy of this pharaoh is his great pyramid on the plain of Giza.

believed to have been created for the sarcophagus of the king, a project that for some unknown reason was not carried out.

The horizontal corridor leads to an exceptional structure, a true masterwork of engineering: the Grand Gallery, a corridor some 47 metres long, 2 metres wide and over 8 metres high, with a corbelled vault. The functions of this part of the building are still mysterious and hard to interpret. It is not clear why the architects felt it was necessary to build such a complex structure simply to transport the wooden coffin to be placed in the sarcophagus. The Grand Gallery leads to a narrow passage followed by a small room, a vestibule that leads to the burial chamber, the entry to which had been blocked by slabs of granite. The King's Chamber, completely faced with granite, is underneath the so-called relieving chambers. These are a series of empty spaces that served to lessen the incredible weight bearing on the structure from above. A sarcophagus was found in the King's Chamber: its size suggests that it was positioned in the room before the construction of the pyramid was completed. When it was discovered the

Drawing of the pyramid of Khufu (from R. Schulz, M. Seidel, *Egypt*, Cologne 1998, p. 63, fig. 33).

Relieving chambers
Aeration ducts
Vestibule
Grand Gallery
Aeration ducts
Aeration ducts
Crypt
King's chamber
Upward shaft
Entrance
Downward shaft
Queen's chamber
Service shaft
Underground chamber

Opposite: North face of the pyramid of Khufu, with the original entrance situated at a height of 15 metres, surmounted by a double arch. The opening made by caliph Al-Ma'mūn, currently used by tourists to enter the building, is somewhat lower.

Granite sarcophagus in the burial chamber of the pyramid of Khufu, c. 2570 BC, Giza. When it was found, the sarcophagus had no cover: it was probably destroyed during the raids on the tomb over the centuries.

sarcophagus, made out of a single piece of red granite, was without a cover: it had probably been opened during one of the numerous desecrations of the pyramid over time. In the relieving chambers there are traces of inscriptions with the name of the pharaoh to whom the monument was dedicated.

The pyramid
of Khufu
with the tomb
of the dignitary
Seshemnefer in
the foreground.

The immense
mass of the
pyramid towers
over the
surrounding
buildings.

The Funerary Complex of Khufu and the Tomb of Hetepheres

The pyramid of Khufu stood at the centre of a traditionally organized funerary complex. The valley temple was located a short distance from the Nile, where the purification and embalming rituals were performed.

After being landed on the west bank of the river, the body was first washed to purify it while a special liturgy was celebrated to enable the dead king, now divine, to enter the sacred area of the complex. This ceremony was performed in what was called the purification tent: the holes for the tent poles and gutters to drain away the water used during the ablutions have been found near the valley temple.

A causeway for processions led from the valley temple to the funerary temple,

adjacent to the pyramid. Along the way they cut and constructed tunnels that are identical to the Grand Gallery inside the pyramid. It has been suggested that it represented a sort of scale model that the technicians used to complete their work.

Within the complex enclosure there are three small pyramids adjacent to the main one. In the southernmost of these, archaeologist François Auguste Mariette found a *stele* that attributed the construction to Henutsen, daughter of Sneferu, wife and half-sister of Khufu. During the 21st Dynasty she was revered as Isis 'the lady of the pyramids', and her chapel was enlarged at that time. The tomb of Hetepheres, mother of Khufu, was also excavated inside the enclosure around this building: no pyramid was built for her. Her tomb was however very lavish and richly furnished.

The fine alabaster sarcophagus that should have

View of the El-Giza archaeological area: in the foreground, a Moslem cemetery; in the background, the pyramids of Menkaura, Khafre and Khufu.

Gold vessels from the tomb of Queen Hetepheres at Giza, c. 2580 BC, Egyptian Museum, Cairo. The tomb of this queen, the mother of Khufu, was richly furnished and also contained an empty sarcophagus of alabaster. Her mummy was probably laid close to that of her husband Sneferu at Dahshur.

contained the mummy was found empty. It was speculated that the queen had been buried next to her husband Sneferu in the pyramid at Dahshur and that her body had been lost during violations of the site.

Then Khufu would have had her funerary furnishings interred in this new tomb, including among many other things a vase containing her mummified entrails. The tombs of all the other relatives of the king and the court were situated around the principal monument.

The Great Pyramid cast its shadow over them so that, symbolically, the pharaoh continued to exercise his control over them even after death.

tomb of Queen
Hetepheres at
Giza, c. 2580 BC,
Egyptian
Museum, Cairo.
It is thought
that Khufu
transferred
the tomb
furnishings of
his mother to
the new tomb.

False door
from the tomb
of Princess
Nefertiabet
at Giza,
c. 2570 BC,
Louvre, Paris.
She was
probably a sister
of Khufu.

The Solar Boat

In 1954, south of the pyramid of Khufu, 41 large slabs of stone were discovered during road building. They evidently served as a covering for a hall underneath.

Archaeologists lost no time: they immediately perceived that the space must have contained something significant that might help them to answer many of the questions that surrounded the Great Pyramid.

The discovery was sensational even though it did not actually resolve any of the mysteries. Underneath the accurately laid stone slabs there was an enormous boat. The excavation required 18 months of work but at the end 1,224 pieces of cedar of Lebanon had been recovered.

The wood was perfectly conserved after so many

centuries thanks to a constant temperature of 22° and relative humidity of 88 per cent. The boat had five oars on each side, and measured 43.4 metres long and 5.9 metres across, and weighed 45 tonnes. The stern and bow were decorated with a spiral papyrus motif; at the centre there was a cabin with decorative columns and a canopy in front.

Tombs in the form of boats were widespread during the Old Kingdom. Examples have been found near the pyramids and also near mastabas. These were actually graves (although no bodies have ever been found) excavated in bedrock or built of unbaked bricks, in shape of a boat.

The structure of Khufu's boat is the same as all the riverboats that navigated in Egypt, where the Nile was the principal means of travel.

The essential significance of the boat and its function in the funerary context can only be suggested at present. According to the oldest beliefs,

Large pit near the pyramid of Khufu, c. 2560 BC, Giza.
The pit contained a large boat: it may have been used in the funeral rites or may have been a symbol of the pharaoh's voyage into the afterlife.

the god Ra owned two boats that he used every day on his solar journey. The boat found at Giza may therefore represent the boat, which would permit the pharaoh to accompany the god after death. However, similar boats have been found in tombs of court officials, who were not entitled to the privilege of accompanying the god across the heavens.

According to other theories, these boats were used during the rituals of the funeral ceremonies to transport the body to the west bank of the river, or may have had a 'terrestrial' purpose, that is they would have been used by the deceased during his visits to the earth and the places he had loved. Here is a new riddle to, add to the long list already waiting for answers.

As it is impossible to resolve the question, it is easier to shut one's eyes and imagine the pharaoh aboard his richly appointed river boat as he navigates among the clouds, accompanied by his court and guided by Ra, as the formula engraved on the pyramids of the Fifth dynasty, the so-called Pyramid texts, reads: 'He navigates the heavens with your boat, oh Ra. And he travels to the earth in your boat, oh Ra.

Now, when you leave by the horizon he is there with his sceptre in hand, like the pilot of your boat, oh Ra'.

Khufu's boat, from Giza, c. 2560 BC, Boat Museum, Giza. The structure is identical to those used on the Nile.

Model of a boat
with rowers,
Middle Kingdom
(2055-1650 BC),
Vatican Palaces,
Rome.
The Nile was
the principal
route for
communications
in Egypt.

The Usurper

According to the Turin royal list, a papyrus written between 1290 and 1224 BC during the reign of Rameses II, Djedefra was Khufu's successor. The lack of information about him suggests that he was a singular and controversial figure, evidently unwelcome in the official chronicles. Djedefra was, in fact, the son of Khufu and a Libyan woman. This 'impurity' inevitably meant that he was entitled to fewer rights than his siblings born of Egyptian women. Djedefra coolly murdered his brother Kanab (the first-born son and legitimate heir to the throne), took his place on the throne and remained there for eight years. His exclusion from the official chronicles of power is confirmed by the fact that he had his pyramid built, not at Giza as might be expected, but eight kilometres away, at Abu Roash. In addition, as if to emphasize his isolation, no tombs of royal family members were erected around his monument. Khafre, a brother of Djedefra but born of an Egyptian mother, ordered his death and, immediately thereafter, to smash all of his statues for the obvious purpose of erasing him completely from public memory. Power thus returned to the hands of the 'pure' Egyptian dynasty.

Traces of Tomb Raiders

Despite all the precautions that the Egyptian kings used to avoid violation and spoliation, the pyramid of Khufu was attacked as early as the First Intermediate Period (2160-2055 BC).

The chamber where the sarcophagus was found had been sealed, after the deposition, with the usual slab of granite, concealed behind a block of limestone like the exterior facing, and the same procedure had been used for the passageways that led from the Grand Gallery to the two corridors (ascending and descending). All these security measures were removed during the period mentioned above, but after the desecration, were re-installed so skilfully that Caliph Al-Ma'mūn did not realize what had occurred. The thieves of the Intermediate Period had entered through the main entrance and were probably deceived by the subterfuge of the builders of the Great Pyramid. Having followed the descending corridor, they arrived at the lower chamber and found it empty. Naturally, they did not stop searching and so, even though the pyramid architects had hidden the entrance that led from the descending corridor to the Grand Gallery, the raiders found it and thus succeeded in reaching the chamber of the sarcophagus. Thus it was that the caliph, who visited these places much, much later, was very disappointed with the results of his incursions.

Opposite:
View of the interior of the great pyramid of Khufu, c. 2570 BC, Giza. The pyramid was raided repeatedly from ancient times.

In His Father's Shadow.
The Pyramid of Khafre

Pyramid
of Khafre,
c. 2570 BC,
Giza. Although
slightly smaller
than that of
Khufu, this
pyramid seems
to be larger
because it is
situated on a
slight natural
rise.

Among the many famous examples of sons wishing to emulate the glory of their fathers, the case of Khufu's son Khafre was, to say the least, unusual.

The story goes that Khufu obliged him to promise that he would build a smaller pyramid than his father's. Khafre, torn between the obligation to be faithful to his vow and the desire not to appear to be less powerful than his parent, found an ingenious expedient. He built a smaller pyramid than Khufu, but positioned it on a natural hill, which raised it up 10 metres and made it appear to be higher.

The building actually measures 143.50 metres in height and 215.16 metres along each base and so is about 3 metres lower and 15 metres shorter on each side than Khufu's pyramid. However, the slope is slightly steeper, about 52.20°, which also makes it appear to be higher.

Despite the fact that the structure soon suffered from spoliation under Rameses II, when blocks were carried away for buildings under construction at Memphis, the upper part still has much of its original limestone facing.

The pyramid originally had two entrances, both on the

north face. One of these leads to an unfinished burial chamber, perhaps as a result of a change of plans during construction, or because it had a purely ritual function: here again mystery reigns. The upper entrance leads to a corridor completely faced with granite, which in turn leads to the stone gate of the second burial chamber, excavated in the bedrock and covered with a gable roof.

It was here that Belzoni found the sarcophagus, completely embedded in the floor up to the cover, with all external and internal surfaces accurately polished. Aside from the cover, which had been broken into two pieces during previous tomb raids, it all seemed to be in perfect condition. The aspiration to make the sensational discovery of the pharaoh's body seemed almost a certainty at that point. But the coffin contained only the bones of a cow and a bull: once again a new discovery only served to create a new mystery.

Statuette of Khafre in black basalt, from Giza, c. 2540 BC, Egyptian Museum, Cairo. The pharaoh's mummy has never been found and inside his sarcophagus, previously raided, were only cattle bones.

The Sphinx:
an Enigmatic Colossus

The Great
Sphinx of Giza,
c. 2540 BC.
This famous
monument
was created
by sculpting
a natural
outcropping
of stone
that remained
after blocks
for the pyramid
of Khufu
had been
quarried.

It is easy to understand that Khufu, in exacting the oath from his son not to build a larger pyramid than his own, intended to maintain his insuperable glory for posterity through the unique monument he had built. But Khafre's desire to go one better was too strong: he not only did everything possible to ensure that his pyramid did not appear to be smaller than his father's, but went further and erected a monument that ensured his own eternal fame, the enormous Sphinx that has been watching over the Plain

of Giza with its cold glance for centuries. Many times, beginning as early as the period of the New Kingdom, it has been threatened by annihilation by the desert winds, which almost buried it in the sands.

This monument came about almost by chance. When Khufu's pyramid was finished, a sort of mound of rock remained standing where limestone blocks had been quarried below the Giza Plain, measuring about 80 metres in length and 20 metres in height.

Under Khafre this mass of stone was transformed into the mysterious form of an animal, a seated lion with forepaws stretched out and an anthropomorphic head. The original nucleus was smoothed, finished with a thick layer of plaster and painted a dark ochre colour, while the face was sculpted to represent the pharaoh with his royal headdress (*nemes*) and ritual beard, fashioned from blocks of limestone. The final result was this colossal stone statue, 57 metres long, with an enigmatic appearance that originated a whole series of legends.

But what did the Sphinx actually represent and what functions did it have? The Sphinx is an image of the king that unites his human, divine and animal natures, represented with the force of the lion. During the New Kingdom it was assimilated with the god Horemakhet, or

The Sphinx of Giza, detail, c. 2540 BC. The enigmatic face of the sphinx spawned many legends about its purpose and the function of the pyramids themselves.

The Dream Stele

During the period of the New Kingdom, under the reign of Amenhotep II, the Sphinx took on a semi-divine role as a consequence of its role as protector, and this role was consolidated during the reign of Thutmose IV, which followed. One of the principle signs of its new importance is a stele or commemorative tablet, known as the Dream Stele, 3 metres high and weighing 15 tonnes, that Thutmose IV had erected between the front paws of the creature. It tells the story of an event that happened to the king when he was young: tired after an exhausting hunt, he fell asleep near the colossus. A strange creature with a human face and the body of a lion appeared to him and begged him to free it of the sand that was suffocating it, and promised that he would become the pharaoh of Egypt in place of the legitimate heir, his brother the first-born son. Thutmose then used all of his energies to resolve the problem and even built a wall to prevent the sand from surrounding the statue. Shortly thereafter his brother died in an attack that has remained shrouded in mystery. Thutmose, crowned pharaoh, had had the promise made to him come true and he decided to venerate the statue with the Greek name of Harmakhis, establishing a cult that became very popular.

Horus: its orientation toward the sun inspired the conviction that it was related to the solar cult. However, it seems that its true function was to guard the tomb of the king by keeping raiders away. This would seem to be confirmed by the declaration that a later period attributed to the statue, as follows: 'I protect the sanctuary of your tomb, I protect your crypt, I banish the stranger who attempts to enter, I fell your enemies with their own arms, I chase away the wicked from the funeral chapel of your tomb, I destroy your enemies in their dens so they may never come out.'

The role of the Sphinx grew in importance during the New Kingdom. It became an element of military iconography, and was believed to go into battle with the king and fight beside his chariot against the enemies.

The Sphinx of Giza is quite different from the famous creature of Greek mythology.

In the story of Oedipus, the Sphinx is a monster with the head and bosom of a woman, the body of a lion and the wings of a bird. It was clearly a creature of female sex, while Khafre's statue is male and does not have the characteristics of cruelty that distinguish the Theban sphinx.

In 1925 a monumental temple, also dated to the 4th Dynasty, was discovered opposite the forepaws of the statue. It consisted of an open court surrounded by a portico of pillars carved in the limestone wall of the quarry.

The temple had no facings on the exterior, but was lavishly faced with alabaster, granite and Tura limestone inside; an altar for offerings was situated at the centre of the court.

Jean-Auguste-Dominique Ingres, *Oedipus and the Sphinx*, Louvre, Paris. In Greek mythology the sphinx is a female creature, with the face and bust of a woman, the body of a lion and wings of a bird.

The Pyramid of Good King Menkaura

Menkaura triad, from Giza, c. 2520 BC, Egyptian Museum, Cairo.

According to Herodotus, Menkaura was a just ruler but he died prematurely.

The reign of Khafre was followed by that of Menkaura, the last pharaoh to build his pyramid on the Giza Plain. Herodotus writes of him as a just ruler, who re-opened the temples closed during the reign of Khufu, his grandfather, permitted the population to dedicate their energies to their own work, freed them from their heavy duties to the sovereign, and ruled so honestly that the Greek historian reported that 'he not only judged fairly, but to anyone who complained about the verdict he gave something of his own'.

His life, however, was not without a stain. Menkaura fell in love with his daughter and possessed her against her will; the girl reacted by hanging herself and the father never overcame his grief. The story said that after this grievous event, an oracle had predicted only six more years of life for Menkaura. The pharaoh then 'had many lamps made and as soon as the night came had them all lit, then he drank and pursued amusements, not stopping during the day or the night [...]. He had devised this so that his years would be twelve instead of six'. His pyramid is the smallest of the complex: it was originally 65.5 metres high, with a base of 105 metres along each side and a slope of 51.25°.

The ancient Arab writers called this the *Mualana* or painted pyramid, probably because the exterior was faced with the pink granite of Aswan. The internal organization follows the traditional principles: two entrances lead, through corridors, to two different chambers: one excavated in the underground bedrock, where Howard Vyse made his findings, and the other constructed higher up. This second chamber had a decorated facade like a monumental palace entrance, with grooves at the sides of the doors: their function has never been fully understood by archaeologists. The funeral complex of Menkaura was also decidedly smaller than those of his predecessors; it was not completed by the pharaoh, but by his son Shepseskaf, a fact, which confirms what, Herodotus told about the brevity of the king's life.

Pyramid of Menkaura, c. 2520 BC, Giza. The pharaoh who succeeded Khafre built the smallest of the three pyramids.

FROM THE GOLDEN AGE OF GIZA TO THE MIDDLE KINGDOM

The epoch of monumental construction on the Giza Plain terminated with Menkaura. His successor, Shepseskaf, did not even build a pyramid for himself, but a humbler mastaba. Times had changed and so, even when the pharaohs of the 5th Dynasty returned to building pyramids, the ancient splendour of the predecessors' constructions could not be equalled.

The pyramids of the 5th Dynasty lacked the lavish setting of the originals, and they were built with inferior quality materials and using less refined techniques. Userkaf, the first king of the dynasty, built at Saqqara and all the later kings built at Abusir. Their temples, decorated with refined reliefs, did not begin to equal, let alone surpass, the splendour of the earlier solar temples.

The 6th Dynasty marked the end of the Old Kingdom. There were many reasons for the crisis: political, economical and climatic. The factors that contributed to the collapse of the dynasty included the weakening of the central powers, the enormous outlay of economic and human resources dedicated to building great works of architecture, and climatic variations that provoked drought and famine.

A long period of crisis followed, characterized by a state of anarchy throughout the kingdom. According to Manetho, during the 7th Dynasty there were 70 kings within 70 days.

The situation returned to normal only under the kings of Thebes of the 11th Dynasty: Mentuhotep II, the pharaoh who united Egypt again, marks the beginning of the period that scholars call the Middle Kingdom. The wisdom of this new king, who reigned for 51 years, enabled the nation to recover the prosperity of ancient times. He also

Opposite: Pyramid of Userkaf, c. 2490 BC, Saqqara. The successors of Menkaura abandoned the extravagant funerary complexes of the preceding period and adopted solutions that were smaller and easier to construct.

dedicated great resources to the construction of a splendid funeral complex at Deir El-Bahari, and many temples.

The consolidation of central power, begun by Mentuhotep, was continued by Amenemhat I, who transferred the capital from Memphis to Thebes, in homage to the origins of the new reigning dynasty. The economy and the arts once again flourished under these rulers: sensational projects were undertaken in the years following the reign of Amenemhat, such as the drainage of the Fayyum swamp area, about 80 kilometres south of Memphis where, after reclamation of the land, sacred buildings and a city called Dja were built.

The Middle Kingdom came to an end, for the first time in the history of Egypt, under the rule of a woman, Queen Sobekneferu, who had reigned for only three years.

A new period of economic crisis lasting as long as 250 years followed her reign.

Pharaoh Mentuhotep II, statue from Deir El-Bahari, 2005-2004 BC, Egyptian Museum, Cairo. This pharaoh came to power after a period of crisis, and reunited the kingdom.

Amenemhet III
portrayed as god
of the Nile in
a double statue
from Tanis,
c. 1831-1786 BC,
Egyptian
Museum, Cairo.

Sarcophagus
of Ashayet, detail
showing the
deceased
receiving
offerings, from
Deir El-Bahari,
c. 2030 BC,
Egyptian
Museum, Cairo.
During the
Middle Kingdom,
Egypt recovered
its ancient
splendour but
this period was
again followed
by an era of
decline.

Statue of a scribe
from Saqqara,
c. 2600-2300 BC,
Louvre, Paris.
The artistic
principles
established
during the Old
Kingdom became
the basis for
the arts in later
periods.

ART OF THE OLD KINGDOM

Woman making beer, 5th Dynasty (2494-2345 BC), Archaeological Museum, Florence. Most of the artistic production of this period comes from funerary contexts.

During the five centuries of the Old Kingdom, a symbolic language developed and formed the foundation of all the artistic creations of the dynasties that followed.

During this long period, art was conceived principally as a way of showing religious ideas, inspired by the same principles that had led to the construction of the pyramids: an unending aspiration to reach beyond the human dimension into the realm of eternity. The Egyptian creations were not, of course, conceived as works of art in themselves, but had distinct functions of their own. Most of the sculptures and paintings that have survived come from religious or funerary contexts, and had been positioned deep inside the temples or the tombs exclusively for the use of the gods or the pharaohs (or other deceased), or to represent their deeds eternally and thus guarantee their immortality.

Sacrificial stone panel showing the god Huti from Saqqara, c. 2500 BC, Egyptian Museum, Cairo. The scenes in bas-relief are usually related to the religious cults and are accompanied by hieroglyphic inscriptions.

Paintings and Reliefs

Egyptian painters were educated in workshops at the palaces or the temples, where they learned the rigid concepts that would guide their work. Painting, in Egypt, was akin to writing, in the sense that it served to relate episodes of the earthly life or afterlife of the pharaoh through descriptions that were clear and comprehensible. The events of the narrative were set out in strips or tiers, with the pharaoh depicted in the main strip, larger than the other human figures, alone or in the company of deities. The other figures, often without any distinguishing characteristics, were depicted in the secondary strips.

The rules that governed the bas-reliefs were completely similar to those of painting, as may be observed in the oldest examples such as the Narmer tablet. There were

Birds in the swamp, bas-relief from the funerary temple of the pyramid of Userkaf at Abusir, 2490 BC, Egyptian Museum, Cairo.

False door of Iri, Old Kingdom (2686-2160 BC), Vatican Palaces, Rome. The deceased is depicted at the centre, seated opposite the offerings.

two techniques available, depending on the effect to be obtained: the bas-relief, with figures that emerged from the background by removing the stone around them; the engraved figures that were sculpted by removing the volumes of the figures from the flat stone. The most common themes of the relief scenes were the rituals of the royal jubilees or conversations between the pharaoh and the gods, while inside the tombs scenes of daily life or funeral rites were represented.

Male profile, polychrome relief, Old Kingdom (2686-2160 BC), Vatican Palaces, Rome. In this case the bas-relief was cut into the stone.

Detail of geese
from a fresco
from the tomb
of Nefermaat
and his wife Itet
at Meidum,
c. 2613-1589 BC,
Egyptian
Museum, Cairo.

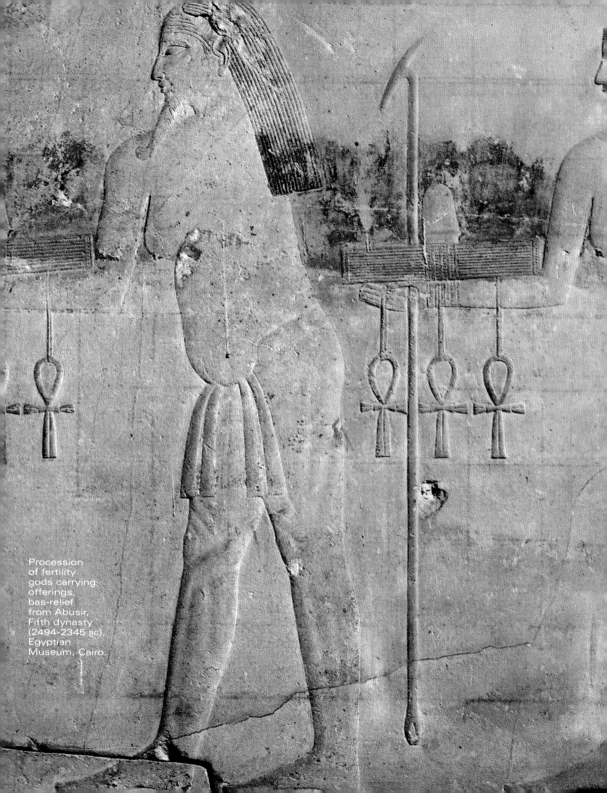

Procession
of fertility
gods carrying
offerings,
bas-relief
from Abusir,
Fifth dynasty
(2494-2345 BC),
Egyptian
Museum, Cairo.

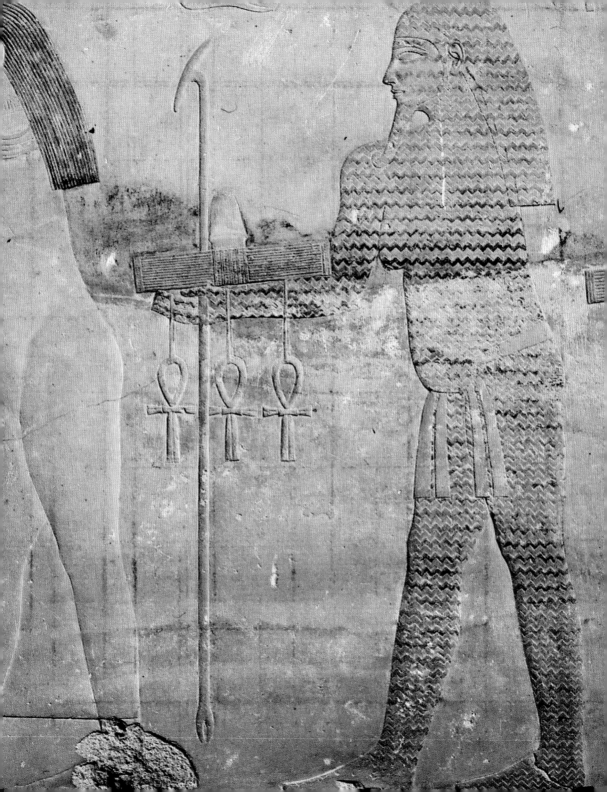

Reserve Heads

A collection of so-called 'reserve' heads made of limestone have been found in the mastabas around the Giza pyramids. Placed near the burial chambers, these heads are life-size but without hair or ears, are completely without any indication of the sex of the figure they represent, and do not seem to be intended for statues. In some respects they are quite realistic, although in others they seem to be stylized. Some scholars believe they were intended to substitute for the head of the mummy, in case it should be lost; others believe they may have served to make funeral masks for the mummy after the mummification process was completed. This would explain the lack of ears, the absence of colour and their mixture of naturalism and idealism.

Reserve head, c. 2550-2500 BC, Egyptian Museum, Cairo.

Sculpture

Egyptian sculpture was conceived within the same rigid framework as paintings and reliefs. The statues, whether made of more or less precious types of stone or wood, were considered to be incarnations of the subject represented and they were given life and power by the engraved names of the person represented and magical formulas. During the 3rd Dynasty the iconography of the human figure was defined in a very detailed way, although these rules were originally applied only to the representation of the pharaoh. There were just seven poses that could be used to represent the king,

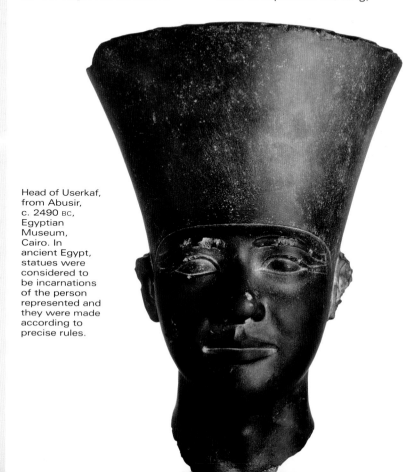

Head of Userkaf, from Abusir, c. 2490 BC, Egyptian Museum, Cairo. In ancient Egypt, statues were considered to be incarnations of the person represented and they were made according to precise rules.

all of which emphasized his political role and divine nature: the most common of these showed the king either sitting or standing with his left foot slightly forward. In the temples the pharaoh was usually depicted accepting offers of the daily cult, standing with arms stretched and hands resting on his kilt, or in adoration of the gods, kneeling with vases in his hands. The attributes of royalty were frequently represented: the king always wore a crown, the royal headdress (*nemes*) and, less frequently, a wig with the uraeus; his clothing could include a short kilt or a triangular loincloth. Other symbols were evidently optional, such as the false beard and regalia including the crook and the flail. From the 3rd Dynasty, private citizens also began to place effigies of their own images inside their tombs, to benefit from the cult offerings like the pharaohs.

Statue of Hetepdief, from Memphis, c. 2630 BC, Egyptian Museum, Cairo. The kneeling position was used for worship.

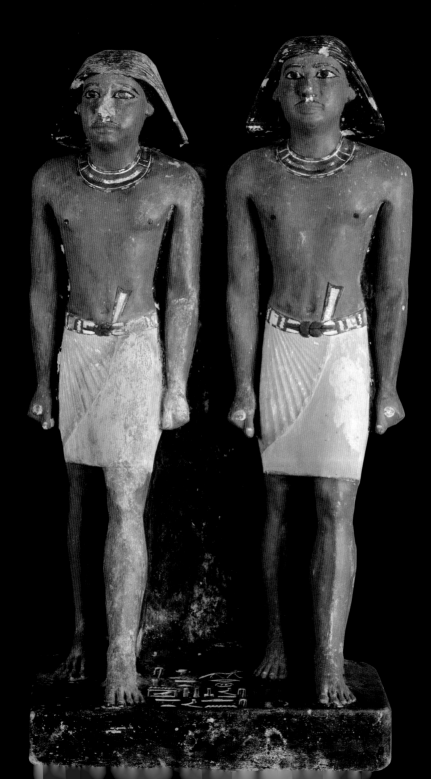

Double statue
of Nimaatsed
from Saqqara,
5th Dynasty
(c. 2494-2345 BC),
Egyptian
Museum,
Cairo. Like
the pharaohs,
ordinary citizens
also placed their
own portraits
in their tombs
to be able to
receive the
benefits of the
funerary cults.

The dwarf Seneb with his family, from Giza, c. 2560 BC, Egyptian Museum, Cairo. Spouses are usually portrayed as they exchange affectionate gestures, with their arms around each others' shoulders.

ART OF THE MIDDLE KINGDOM

Egyptian art was always intimately related to the political and historical events of the nation at the time it was created.

The first artworks of the Middle Kingdom used a schematic style that seemed to have lost all contact with the splendours of the Old Kingdom, but the ancient magnificence was completely recovered by the 12th Dynasty. The new artists demonstrated their proficiency, especially in sculpture and reliefs characterized by great attention to detail and naturalness, and in the wall paintings of the tombs characterized by greater attention to colour.

In the production of sculpture for private citizens, a new iconography appeared: the block statue, which represents the subject seated on the ground with legs drawn up to the chest and arms crossed on the knees, surrounded by a mantle that left only the head, the hands and feet in view.

Architecture did not produce anything comparable to the great constructions on the Giza Plateau. However important works were carried out, such as the oasis of Fayyum. Here Amenemhat III, a king of the 12th Dynasty, built a temple to the cobra goddess Renenutet and the crocodile god Sobek, the walls of which are decorated with scenes of the king accompanied by his son as they make offerings to the gods. Amenemhat also built a pyramid for himself, with a completely different appearance to those of the 4th Dynasty.

The funerary temple, called a 'labyrinth' by ancient writers,

Statue of Senusret III (Sesostris III), 1870-1831 BC, Louvre, Paris. The artists of the Middle Kingdom achieved great naturalness in their sculptures.

had 3,000 rooms where 12 crocodiles lived, in homage to the principal divinity revered by the pharaoh.

During the Middle Kingdom a new type of column capital appeared. It was decorated on two sides with the head of the goddess Hathor, and was often imitated later. Among the minor arts the extremely refined gold and silver jewellery with set stones of cornelian, turquoise, lapis lazuli and glass paste of many colours found in the tombs of princesses indicate that the goldsmith's craft was highly developed.

The rebirth of artistic splendour during the Middle Kingdom was followed by a period of decadence that accompanied internal disturbances throughout Egypt for another interval of about two centuries, until the appearance of the New Kingdom, when the nation achieved an unprecedented level of prosperity. At this time, as a direct consequence of this wellbeing, Egyptian art reached the apex of its development.

Senmut and Neferure, block statue from Karnak, c.1470 BC, Egyptian Museum, Cairo.

This type of statue was the most original invention of the art of the Middle Kingdom.

THE SITE TODAY

Opposite:
View of the Nile
at sunset. The
principal sites
of Egyptian
civilization are
located along
the river.

Under the burning sun of the desert, the immortal Egyptian civilization left its mark on the left bank of the Nile: Saqqara, with the oldest stone building in Egypt and evocative Giza with its stone giants.

Altogether there are actually 87 pyramids along the 160-kilometre strip of land that stretches from Giza to El-Lahun in Lower Egypt. Visited by countless explorers, enthusiasts and admirers, these sites continue to harbour their secrets.

The magnificence of the pyramids is almost blinding outside, while the mysterious and rarefied atmosphere inside has maintained its spell through the centuries.

Archaeology at Saqqara

Opposite:
Royal pavilion
from Djoser's
funerary
complex,
c. 2650 BC,
Saqqara.
The cult of
the pharaoh
celebrated its
rites in these
structures.

Saqqara, named after Sokar the god of fertility, is located on the left bank of the Nile about 25 kilometres south of Cairo. It is the largest necropolis in Egypt: between 800 and 1,800 metres wide and 8 kilometres long. The principal phases of the evolution of royal tombs are represented here, from Djoser's pyramid to Coptic monuments. The area is divided into two sectors: the northern sector extends toward Abusir, while the southern sector extends toward Dahshur. The entrance to the complex is embellished by palm groves, but these quickly give way to the desert that surrounds the step pyramid, the heart of the whole complex. From this point there are no obstacles to interrupt the view as far as the magnificent pyramids of Giza. Located in the northern sector of Saqqara, the genial architect Imhotep built a wall some 10.5

metres high around Djoser's pyramid, which imitated the facade of the royal palace, with 14 false doors. The real entrance led into a hypostyle hall, reconstructed by Jean Philippe Lauer by repositioning some 2,000 stone fragments, fluted to imitate wooden columns. On the left, south of the complex, the visitor can observe another ingenious invention of Imhotep, the Cobra Wall that decorates a wall of the south tomb: the sacred serpents of the goddess Wadjet are depicted above the false doors, where only the deceased could pass when he came to collect the offerings dedicated to him. The court and the pavilion where the jubilee ritual of *Heb-Sed* was celebrated are situated to the right of the entrance, with chapels that imitate the halls used to celebrate the festivities of Predynastic Egypt, followed immediately by the houses of North and

South, two symbolic buildings characterized by columns that were originally 12 metres high (though today they only stand to three metres). The last building along this path is the 'cellar' (*serdab*), where the oldest life-size Egyptian statue was found, now conserved in the Cairo Museum. It depicts the beneficiary of all this magnificence, King Djoser, seated here to spy, through two holes in the facade of the building, on the offerings being made in his honour in the adjacent funerary temple.

You can only look at the first pyramid in Egyptian history from the outside: the building is closed because of the danger of collapse. The entrance was on the north side and led to the series of chambers that characterized the interior. On the south side the traces of the tunnel opened during the 26th Dynasty are quite visible. Although it is not known whether the purpose of the tunnel was to plunder or to explore, it is certain that a thousand square metres of blocks were removed at that time. Visitors to this extraordinary site can continue to visit the less famous but just as fascinating pyramids of Djoser's successor Sekhemkhet, and the kings of the 5th and 6th Dynasties, together with an impressive number of mastabas and noble tombs.

Relief of Sneferu from Saqqara, Ägyptisches Museum und Papyrussamlung, Berlin.

Walls of Djoser's funerary complex, c. 2650 BC, Saqqara. The magnificence of these buildings gave the architect Imhotep, who designed the whole complex, enduring fame.

Statue of Khafre in black basalt, left side and front, c. 2540 BC, Egyptian Museum, Cairo. This pharaoh is one of the three to have chosen the plain of Giza to erect his pyramid.

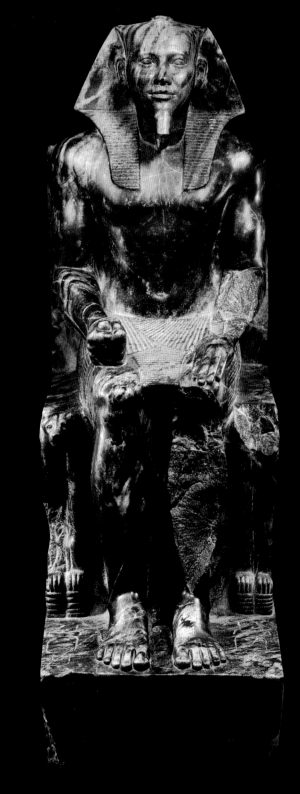

El-Ahram, the Giza Plain

El-Ahram, 'the pyramids', this is the name used by Egyptians for the Giza Plain, known in ancient times as *Imentet*, 'the West', or *Kher neter*, 'the necropolis'. Located 12 kilometres west of Cairo, the sandy plateau chosen by the pharaohs of the 4th Dynasty lies on the left bank of the Nile, at the end of the boulevard to the pyramids which starts in the crowded neighbourhood of the same name.

The visit to the buildings starts at the entrance to the oldest and most famous of the site, the pyramid of Khufu. The modern entrance is from the north and leads to the Grand Gallery, by way of a tunnel excavated by raiders. This leads directly to the King's Chamber, where the sarcophagus can be admired, without its mummy however.

The principal building is surrounded by the ruins of the rich funeral complex of Khufu. East of the pyramid, in addition

The pyramids of Giza, c. 2570-2520 BC. This site is situated west of Cairo and hosts the tombs of the 4th Dynasty.

to the remains of the funerary temple, there are three pits for solar boats, each of which contains a boat for the king's travels during his afterlife. There are also three satellite pyramids, one of which has been attributed to Henutsen, daughter of Sneferu and also wife and half-sister of Khufu.

The necropolis to the east of the pyramid was reserved for high-ranking dignitaries, the tombs of the members of the royal family, including Khufu's mother, queen Hetepheres, and those of the king's followers.

Among the numerous mastabas only a few are open to the public today. Another necropolis is located to the west, where the king's vizier, Hemon, is buried.

Along the ceremonial avenue that connects these buildings with the valley temple, there are ruins of a wall of basalt, discovered only in 1994, that was part of a port on the Nile used to transfer the coffin during the ceremonies prior to burial. South of these structures, 1,224 wood fragments were found in two separate cavities: the fragments were laboriously recomposed over ten years of extenuating and painstaking work by Ahmed Youssef Mustapha, to form the large solar boat of the pharaoh. Mustapha, believes that the boat sailed the Nile at least once in a ritual voyage to Abydos, the reign of Osiris, god of the dead. The final result of this patient reconstruction is the splendid and delicate vessel, perfect for navigation, exhibited in a hall built especially for it on the south side of Khufu's pyramid.

The surroundings of the pyramids of Khafre and Menkaura are just as elaborate. At the top of Khafre's pyramid the white limestone pyramidion suggests how blinding the pyramids must have been originally, when they were completely faced with the same type of stone.

The pyramids of Khufu's successors were also surrounded by walls that are still visible, and had satellite pyramids, only one of which is visible near Khafre's tomb. Three are visible near the pyramid of Menkaura; of these

Opposite: Reconstruction drawing of the area of the pyramids of Giza (from Z. Hawass, A. Siliotti, *Piramidi d'Egitto*, Vercelli 2004, p. 47).

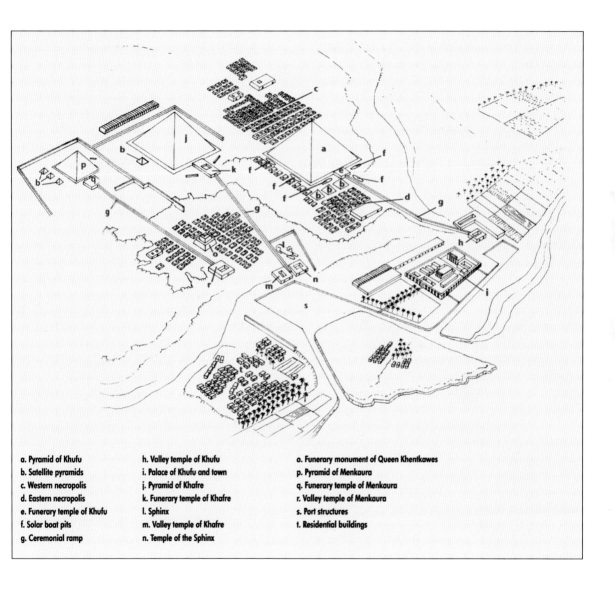

a. Pyramid of Khufu
b. Satellite pyramids
c. Western necropolis
d. Eastern necropolis
e. Funerary temple of Khufu
f. Solar boat pits
g. Ceremonial ramp

h. Valley temple of Khufu
i. Palace of Khufu and town
j. Pyramid of Khafre
k. Funerary temple of Khafre
l. Sphinx
m. Valley temple of Khafre
n. Temple of the Sphinx

o. Funerary monument of Queen Khentkawes
p. Pyramid of Menkaura
q. Funerary temple of Menkaura
r. Valley temple of Menkaura
s. Port structures
t. Residential buildings

the one farthest to the east is attributed to the king's spouse Khamerernebty II.

Of the funeral monuments to these two pharaohs, Khafre's seems to be better preserved, with the remains of its valley temple where, in a small shrine, the cult statue of the pharaoh was found. The structure was next to the temple dedicated to the Sphinx, the guardian of the plain. This enigmatic figure of a seated lion with a human head watches over the destiny of its ancient master from its position at the entrance to the ceremonial avenue that leads to the pyramid. The Arabs called it *Abu el-Hol*, 'the father of terror', but unlike its Greek namesake, who devoured anyone who could not resolve the riddles it proposed, the Sphinx of Giza never killed anyone! Fragments of its beard are conserved in the British Museum in London, while part of the nose is displayed in the museum in Cairo.

This is all that remains of the devastation perpetrated by Mamluks who conducted their military exercises by shooting cannonades aimed precisely at the nose of the statue.

Detail of the *pyramidion* of the pyramid of Khafre, c. 2540 BC, Giza.

The apex of the pyramid is the only part that retains the original facing.

The Sphinx,
c. 2540 BC, Giza.
This famous
monument has
been guarding
the pyramid
of Khafre
for centuries.

View of the entrances to several mastabas of dignitaries, with the pyramid of Khafre in the background, Giza.

King Djoser, statue
from Saqqara,
left side and
front, c. 2650 BC,
Egyptian Museum,
Cairo. The
masterpieces found
in the pyramids
formed one of the
most important
collections in the
museum.

Masterpieces in the Egyptian Museum, Cairo

The collection of the Egyptian Museum in Cairo includes approximately 120,000 pieces, which make it possible to take a fascinating journey backwards through the thousands of years of Egyptian history.

The sections dedicated to the Protodynastic epoch and the Old Kingdom conserve the sensational works of art found in the pyramids or in their vicinity. The statue of King Djoser, discovered in the 'cellar' of his funerary complex, greets visitors to the museum with its imposing presence, still capable of inspiring a sense of reverence.

In the first room on the left, one of the most famous and widely published works of Egyptian art attracts the visitor: the Menkaura triad. Discovered at Giza in the valley temple of the pharaoh, the triad represents Menkaura between the goddess Hathor and the divine personification of the province of Thebes, all three supported by a slab of shale. The incredible sense of movement that characterizes the three figures, in the classic posture with one leg forward, was accentuated in ancient times by the bright colours of the statue which were still visible when it was found, but quickly disappeared.

In the next room, the seated figure of Pharaoh Khafre, sculpted in very hard black basalt, his face imbued with divine serenity in contrast with the vigorous power of the muscles of his chest and arms, is just as impressive. The statue was discovered in the valley temple of the pharaoh, together with numerous other images of him that served, according to the interpretation of scholars, as substitutes of the pharaoh used to receive offerings and to carry out the funeral ceremonies. It is

Detail of the Menkaura triad, from Giza, c. 2520 BC, Egyptian Museum, Cairo. The pharaoh is represented between the goddess Hathor and the personification of a province of Egypt.

a quirk of destiny that the only image to reach us of the most famous of the pharaohs, Khufu, is a little statue only 7.5 centimetres high that represents him holding the ceremonial flail.

Our journey through the marvels of the history of Egypt terminates here, but anyone who is fortunate enough to visit this extraordinary country will continue the museum visit through an incredibly rich series of works of art, an unsurpassable trace of the secrets and mysteries of a people who have remained immortal despite the passage of time and the desert sands.

Khufu, statuette in ivory from Abydos, c. 2570 BC, Egyptian Museum, Cairo.

This small-scale portrait is the only known image of this most famous of the pharaohs.

Detail of statue
of Khafre in
black basalt,
c. 2540 BC,
Egyptian
Museum, Cairo.
This and other
similar statues
represented the
pharaoh himself
in the rituals.

The pyramids
of Giza at
sunset, one
of the most
popular
attractions
for visitors.